Brave New Wave

Brave New Wave

edited by Jack David

Black Moss Press

Copyright © 1978, the authors.

Published by Black Moss Press, po box 143 Station A,
Windsor Ontario. Financial assistance towards the
publication of this book was provided by the Ontario
Arts Council and the Canada Council.

Black Moss Press books are distributed in Canada and
the U.S. by Firefly Books, 2 Essex Avenue, Unit #5,
Thornhill, Ontario. All orders should be directed there.

Designed by Tim Inkster, printed and bound by The
Porcupine's Quill (Erin) in December of 1978. The stock
is Zephyr Antique Laid and the type is Megaron.

ISBN 0-88753-051-6

Contents

Introduction to *Brave New Wave*

Jack David

Twelve years have passed since the publication of Raymond Souster's prophetic anthology, *New Wave Canada: The Explosion in Canadian Poetry* (1966). Containing the poetry of George Bowering, Frank Davey, Daphne Buckle (Marlatt), David McFadden, Michael Ondaatje, and bpNichol, Souster's book marked a significant departure from the past. He contended that the 1950s had been a "largely reactionary decade" that ignored the "most important fact for Canadian poetry, . . . that Canada is situated on the northern border of the United States of America."

Not only did these new poets arise, they grew and flourished amidst an astonishing array of presses, magazines, CanLit courses, government support, and critical attention. No single style or school prevailed, and A.J.M. Smith's carefully chosen phrase describes the result: eclectic detachment. Canadian poets have since been liberated from blindly pursuing trends, and their poems have arrived at distinctiveness more quickly than otherwise might be expected. For an Atwood, an Ondaatje, and a Nichol to spring up in one generation clearly marks the maturation of Canadian poetry.

I have organized the essays by beginning with more traditional poets, then turning to the West Coast, examining the visual and sound poets, and returning to the apparently traditional. The poets were selected because I believe they are each gifted in their own way (Joe Rosenblatt, Victor Coleman, and Gwen MacEwen might well have been included); the essays provide thorough, intelligent, and well-written analyses of the poets' work to date.

I am grateful to the following journals for permission to reprint, in whole or in part, the essays which originally appeared therein: *Essays on Canadian Writing, Studies in Canadian Literature, Open Letter, Lakehead University Review*, and *Canadian Literature*. Thanks also to Press Porcepic for permission to reprint Eli Mandel's essay from *Another Time*.

John Robert Colombo:
Documentary Poet as Visionary

Jean Mallinson

Anne Sexton has said that the poet takes used furniture and turns it into trees. John Robert Colombo, our local literary scavenger, second-hand man, poet of thrift who can turn funeral baked meats into wedding cakes, has discovered the secret that in every page of prose there is a poem crying to be let out. For most poets the *donné*, the thing given, is the world; for Colombo it is the word, the words of other people. His work is a mixture of humility and poised arrogance: he is humble because he knows he needs the words of others to start with, arrogant because he knows he can improve on them. And yet, self-declared and dedicated epigone, pick-pocket, he treats his sources with a respect and tenderness which reveals him to be a responsible man and poet. He does not say: a poor thing, but mine own; he says: a lovely thing, and I got it from someone else.

In his compilations of "found poetry" he has described a circle whose centre is everywhere and whose circumference is nowhere. If the French discovered "found poetry" it is surely appropriate that a North American should claim it for his own — finders, keepers — because it is the most democratic of poetic kinds. Colombo has eschewed the hieratic and redeemed the demotic, the banal, the everyday, the ignored. Collector, beach comber,

13

encyclopedist, arranger, anatomist, compiler of an endless commonplace book, he celebrates the poetry which is
all around us but which we often fail to notice. He wants, he
says, "to turn the immense nonsense that numbs us into
the narrative that haunts us" (*Neo Poems*, 38).

He is in public and by profession the poet as supreme
opportunist, and joyfully exploits instead of lamenting his
position as epigone or, to use Harold Bloom's term,
"belated poet". Of his style he has said, accurately, "There
is a poesy between speech and song. I am much closer to
speech than to song, to prose than to poetry" (*Neo Poems*,
28). Poetry, his endeavours implicitly say, can be picked up
on our own doorstep, like the morning paper.

Yet he is a democrat with a difference, because he is also
a man of lore, who sets up an elaborate and beguiling
apparatus to enshrine the gems his pockets bulge with
after he goes walking in the world of words. Is he an avatar
of Sir Thomas Browne, disguised as the Common Man in
the Street? Or is he really the Common Man in the Street,
with a passion for the arcane which, since he is a man of
words, leads him to elegant and erudite marginalia rather
than to the backrooms of the Free Masons and the
Rosicrucians? Like the Carlos in the name of another
democratic poet, the Colombo in his name suggests
something exotic, esoteric; perhaps it is he who is
responsible for the wit and the recherché lore with which
some of his plain pieces are surrounded, like beach
pebbles set in filigree. There is a delicacy of touch, a sense
of etiquette, finesse, game, to his marginalia; he is never
ponderous. In one footnote he quotes Louis Dudek's
definition of the "found poem":

So the found poem is really a piece of realistic literature, in which significance appears inherent in the
object — either as extravagant absurdity or as unexpected worth. It is like driftwood, or pop art, where
natural objects and utilitarian objects are seen as the
focus of generative form or meaning.

(*Translations from the English*, 8)

Do we detect a tongue in cheek? Do we hear some of Colombo's slighter pieces squirm on the page and say, "Who, me?" The footnote to "Overdue" is, as it was meant to be, disarming:

A confession. "Overdue" is not a found poem but an original poem. Written "in the found manner", it might best be described as pseudo-found or found manqué. "Found" is a style, not a content. One is inclined to believe a found poem. Who believes a sonnet these days? (*Translations*, 11)

As artists do, he praises his own metier, in love with its virtues, which are legion and sometimes timely:

Found art is the most ecological of the arts, for it re-cycles the things of the past. Last year's prose may be this year's poem.
(*Translations*, 21)

The variety of his sources suggests the grab-bag learned-ness of the autodidact or the provincial derailed by reading, but Colombo is nothing if not urbane and his trains run on time. And some of his lore has the immediate effect of making the familiar, strange and fascinating, as when we learn in a footnote that there was "a book popular in Waterloo County, a handbook of spells, chants, curses, incantations, hex signs, recipes and nostrums called *The Sixth and Seventh Book of Moses*" (*Translations*, 37). "Another book of the black arts whispered about in Waterloo County is . . . *Albertus Magnus, Being the Approved, Sympathetic and Natural Egyptian Secrets, or, White and Black Art for Man and Beast: The Book of Nature and the Hidden Secrets and Mysteries of Life Unveiled; Being the Forbidden Knowledge of Ancient Philosophers*" (*Translations*, 42). Our notions of Waterloo County, Ontario, expand and take wings.

As commentary on these pieces he quotes Harold Rosenberg: "If you inhabit a sacred world, you *find* art rather than *make* it" (*Translations*, 42). In another context he cites John Keble: "We should be set to hallow all we see" (*Translations*, 61). And after the little documentary poem "Levitations" Colombo comments: "I like to think that, whenever this poem is read aloud, something, somewhere in the world, levitates" (*Translations*, 91). Is Colombo suggesting that we already live in that sacred world where art is found, rather than made, or is he trying to bring it about by incanting his found poems, which are like rumours or evidence of the existence of that world? When all prose has been redeemed for poetry, that world will exist.

Many of his poems are tributes, little shrines. Often his sources help him, are already at half-way house on the road from prose to poetry. Colombo is frequently playful, he knows that found poetry is often a kind of game, and his best pieces have a quality which Randall Jarrell used to describe the poetry of William Carlos Williams: an "empirical gaiety". In one of his footnotes he quotes Cocteau's imperative, that we should "rehabilitate the commonplace" (*Translations*, 113). Any number can play, the world is full of words waiting to be redeemed, rescued, rearranged. But not everyone has Colombo's eye for the possible, his disciplined restraint, his humble and tender respect for what is already there.

Colombo's recent encyclopedic endeavours, his compilations of Canadian quotations, proverbs, references, are not unrelated to his redemptive action with regard to words. He quotes with approval E.B. White's description of his sense of responsible vocation as a writer:

> As a writing man, or secretary, I have always felt charged with the safekeeping of all the unexpected items of worldly or unworldly enchantment, as though I might be held personally responsible if even a small one were to be lost.
>
> (*Translations*, 71)

By a kind of paradox, the writer as secretary is a safekeeper of secrets not by concealing them, but by recording them, making them public. There is, indeed, a double movement

16

in Colombo's literary action: mysteries are made manifest, available and the commonplace is, if you will, elevated, included within the circle of art. The *gramarye* or glamour, the secret art of words, is turned into grammar, syntax in black on white, words on a plain page; and the grammar of demotic speech has cast over it something of the glamour of poetry.

In the piety of his work as a compiler, Colombo reminds us of Samuel Johnson, and he shares with Johnson a wide and deep sense of the ways in which life imitates art, and words even in the most unlikely contexts imitate literature. Paul Fussell says of Johnson:

> His repeated literary action is that of redeeming the commonplace by showing us how we have misdefined it, how in our snobbery or thoughtlessness we have ignored the possibilities of beauty in what we take to be ordinary things. He shows us how the humblest form can be made the vehicle of the subtlest art.
>
> (*Samuel Johnson: The Life of Writing*, 89)

> Johnson's great art is the art of redeeming the received and even the commonplace. It is entirely typical of his literary procedure for him to take up the commonplace literary (or frequently subliterary) kind, put into it exactly the sort of materials that belong there, . . . and so redeem the ordinary. . . .
>
> (Fussell, 124)

Like Johnson, then, in some of his literary enterprises, his talent for the encyclopedic, and his willingness to act himself, because in doing so he is able both to satisfy public expectations, friendly or hostile, and to hide behind his own masks; Colombo is also like Johnson in his sensitivity to the pervasive influence of genre, convention, expectation and the forms it generates, on every action which is expressed in language. Like Johnson, too, Colombo is a man of schemes and undertakings, a practical bread-and-butter man, who sees gaps and hastens to use all his industry and ingenuity to fill them, who makes people aware of what they wanted all along but didn't know it, by providing them with it.

R.P. Blackmur calls an epiphany a "showing of something that is already made"; in this sense all of Colombo's found poems are epiphanies: showings of things already made, *as* made, framing them, arranging them, so that the artifice latent in them will be manifest. And since, as he says,

Both Time and Place
Take place
Above and Below Art
Rarely Recordedly
As a Part of Art

(*Abracadabra*, 34)

since, in other words, most of life takes place outside literature, his dedicated task is both subversive and inclusive: subversive in that it undermines and enlarges our sense of what is literature and what is not; inclusive in the arc which he describes in order to bring what he calls the orphaned words in.

In the prose epilogue to *Abracadabra* Colombo explains at some length what he thinks he is about in his "translations from the English":

What I really want to do here is to write a poem of documentary realism. . . . Everyday objects are charged with reality; the poet's task is releasing this reality any way he sees fit.

(*Abracadabra*, 124)

He said further in an interview on the CBC that he sees his work not as marginal, but as related to a central Canadian tradition — documentary. In his foreword to the *Mackenzie Poems* he explains:

What was functional has now become aesthetic, or psychologically functional. . . . Such devices edit reality and make our legacy functional.

(*Mackenzie Poems*, 20, 25)

Dorothy Livesay, in her essay "The Documentary Poem: A Canadian Genre", sees the found poems of Colombo and F.R. Scott as part of a tradition which she traces back to such poems as "At the Long Sault", "Malcolm's Katie", "The Wind My Enemy", "Call My People Home" and "The Trial of a City". What interests her, she says, in these developments

> ... is the evidence they present of a conscious attempt to create a dialectic between the objective facts and the subjective feelings of the poet. The effect is often ironic; it is always intensely personal. ... The more the pattern is studied, the more clearly it seems that such poems are not isolated events in Canadian poetry. Rather, they are part of a tradition which has enlivened our English-Canadian literature for a hundred and fifty years.
> (*Contexts of Canadian Criticism*, 267)

Colombo's longer essays in the found manner, like *John Toronto, The Mackenzie Poems*, "The Last Words of Louis Riel", the Norman Bethune poems, are closer to the extended documentary form which Livesay has in mind, but his briefest poems are documentary too in the sense that, though they are complete, shapely, they are illumined and enriched by the context in reality from which they were drawn.

Louis Dudek, with fine panache, said, a number of years ago that

> The chimera of reality, as a prime myth, to be investigated in every joint, hoof, claw, bend, fierce eyelash, lightning glance, is richer than all the myths of barbarous antiquity or of Christianity, . . . the reality glimpsed in the appearance, is a higher vision than any aesthetic or ascetic Paradiso. . . . . by looking at the visible we may discover the invisible.
> (*Delta*, 20, 32)

In similar vein, and with undiminished bravura, he suggested in a recent interview in *Essays on Canadian*

Writing that "the Canadian mythopoeists are not that far from the realists in their subject matter or in the kind of problem they deal with: to transform the empty desolation of Canadian life into art and into human meaning" (*ECW*, No. 3, 2-3). Making allowances for Dudek's Romantic rhetoric, it seems to me that his insight into the convergence of the two often apparently opposed modes in Canadian poetry is a valid one. Colombo's statement that he wants to "turn the immense nonsense that numbs us into the narrative that haunts us" is not so very different; and it seems to me that the two modes meet, precisely, in Colombo's work, with his interest in, on the one hand, the extravagantly arcane, the *gramarye*, the Abracadabra, and on the other, the blisses of the commonplace.

Like Tom Wayman, but with a difference, Colombo is a good citizen of the country of everyday and has "bound himself to this country with an oath so deep/ there is not a dream that is strong enough/ to free him from it" (*For and Against the Moon*, 119). Like Wayman, he is a "reality junkie" but he knows, too, that things as they are are changed on poetry's blue guitar. Colombo is a kind of anthologist, collector, of the songs of the country of everyday, and he shows us that that country, which we live in, is a more varied and miraculous place than we ever dreamed.

Paul West, some years ago, listening for a Canadian voice in poetry and hearing it in some of the poems of W.W.E. Ross, said:

> . . . if you are sufficiently attentive to the real world, a straight account will suffice. . . . What we are given, by . . . Ross . . . is an ideogram which celebrates. This is the raw material chopped up into assimilable pieces, each of which is a cause for wonder. . . . It is a mode [which seeks] . . . to restore us to a sense of primal, unelaborated things. . . . [This is] the mode of spiritual geography in terms of emblems.
>
> (*Contexts of Canadian Criticism*, 208-212)

If you are sufficiently attentive to the real world, a straight account will suffice. And to a man of letters, responsible for the safe keeping of worldly and unworldly enchantment, *only* an account will suffice, because when all is said and done, only what is recorded remains, and the poem, in the end, survives the plum.

The ultimate, unrealizable goal of such documentary, which gives us a spiritual geography in terms of emblems, is to turn all of reality into art, all words into poetry:

I want to anthologize and include in my poems all other poems, all other places, all other things.

(*Neo Poems*, 38)

. . . this literary miscellany . . . which binds humans together, is my and your vulgate version of the visionary world, something to conjure with, a completely human and impromptu poem.

(*Neo Poems*, 83)

What I wish to stress is the mode of inventory — the straight account — as transfiguration, explicit in Colombo and in such a writer as Alice Munro:

And no list could ever hold what I wanted, for what I wanted was every last thing, every layer of speech and thought, stroke of light on bark or walls, every smell, pothole, pain, crack, delusion, held still and held together — radiant, everlasting.

(*Lives of Girls and Women*, 253)

For a visionary documentary writer like Munro the raw material is the world of her experience, for Colombo it is the words of the world which, as Wallace Stevens has said, are the life of the world. But the aim — to celebrate or pay tribute by faithful selection and transcription — is similar.

I think, too, that the Theatre Passe-Muraille, and James Reaney in the Donnelly plays, to cite only two instances, are "making our legacy functional" in terms of documentary which celebrates. And I sense in the work of two contemporary Canadian painters something of the mingling of documentary, wit, playfulness and vision which animates Colombo's work. Alex Wise's paintings, "Courteous Service, 1973", "Exercising Flying Cows Over the Governor-General's Grounds, 1975" and "Northern Wedding Scenes" are fey, witty, local in colour, surreal yet literal, a rendering of the familiar in all its implicit poetry and comedy. The canvasses of Greg Curnoe, too, are local, documentary, characterized by a kind of piety, a faithful rendering, and by a limpid, paint-box use of colour which is both playful and transfiguring.

My remarks about Colombo's place in the Canadian tradition are at best but brief surmise, but if Dorothy Livesay is right in thinking that documentary is a major Canadian mode, we may safely say that the Mona Lisa smile which illuminates the level gaze of the friendly face adorning the dust jackets of most of Colombo's books is not smug or mysterious: it comes from his secure knowledge that, whatever his detractors say, in endlessly elaborating his "vulgate version of the visionary world", he sits at the centre and beholds bright day.

Homage to J (R) C

After Bartlett in the alphabet-Colombo,
Our very own household word,
Explorer, discoverer of treasure-trove
In America's Attic,

Scavenger, second-hand John,
Tag-and-Tome man.

Second-generation John,
Epigone, pick-pocket,
Jewell thief, *filigranist*

Johannes, alchemist,
Sublimator, quintessential man,
Transubstantiating
Prose into poetry.

Arch John,
Peter Quince at the Clavier,
Comedian as the letters COLOMBO,
Frugal, ecological John,
Thrifty stitcher
Of twice-turned words.

Subversive *Juan*, conspirator,
Plotter, scheming for the revolution
When there will be only poems.

Redeemer,
Apocalyptic John,
Harrower of the hell of common speech,
Key turner, jail breaker, knowing
That in every page of prose
There is a poem crying,
'Let me out.'

Nets and Chaos:
The Poetry of Michael Ondaatje

Sam Solecki

My mind is pouring chaos
in nets onto the page.

(" 'the gate in his head' ")[1]

Michael Ondaatje is a poet of reality. In applying this
phrase to Ondaatje I wish to call attention to the fact that in
his poetry the essential nature of experience is consistently being described and examined. The entire thrust of
his vision is directed at compelling the reader to reperceive
reality, to assume an unusual angle of vision from which it
appears (or, more accurately, re-appears) surreal, absurd,
inchoate, dynamic and, most importantly, ambiguous. His
poetic world is filled with mad or suicidal herons, one-eyed
mythic dogs, tortured people, oneiric scenes, gorillas,
dragons, creative spiders and imploding stars. These
extraordinary images function as a kind of metaphoric
shorthand to disorient the reader, to make him enter either
a psychological or material reality which has been
revealed as almost overwhelmingly anarchic or chaotic. At
issue in Ondaatje's work is not just the existence of an
alternate reality but of different perceptions of one which
the reader has always assumed to be clear, patterned and
unambiguously meaningful. To use Wallace Steven's apt
phrase, Ondaatje is a "connoisseur of chaos", and whether

his poems depict an unconscious mode of being similar to Freud's primary process ("Biography", "King Kong", "King Kong meets Wallace Stevens") or simply the ordinary phenomenal flux of life ("Loop", "We're at the graveyard"), the central formal and thematic concern in his work has been the description of internal and external reality as dynamic, chaotic and ambiguous.[2]

But his major poems — among the best of his generation — not only redefine our sense of the real they also create an awareness of the extent to which the mind distorts reality in any act of perception and description. In the period between *The Dainty Monsters* (1967) and *Coming Through Slaughter* (1976) Ondaatje has shown an increasing awareness of the epistemological difficulties involved in the relationship between the "nets" of the perceiving and recreating mind and the "chaos" of life. Not content to raise just the usual issue about the limitations of language as a representational medium, Ondaatje has shown more concern for the possibility that poetry (or art in general) might not be able to do justice to reality's existential complexity either because of the mind's inevitable tendency to see pattern and clarity where life offers only flux and ambiguity, or because of the artist's inability to sustain the intensity of the kind of creativity needed during the creative moment. This tension between mind and chaos is at the centre of Ondaatje's work: its implications can be seen in the binary nature of his imagery, in the deliberate thematic irresolution of his major lyrics, in the complex structuring of his three longer works, and in the fact that each of these has more than one ending. Without resorting to what R.P. Blackmur has termed the fallacy of expressive form,[3] one variant of which can be seen in some of the Black Mountain school and in Victor Coleman's poetry, Ondaatje has written poems describing the fundamentally chaotic nature of experience.

In his first collection, *The Dainty Monsters*, most of the poems simply reflect the assumption that a lyric can recreate any aspect of consciousness or of material reality, or re-enact any experience chosen by the poet. Only in the poems about poetry, "Four Eyes", "The Martinique", and

"Eventually the Poem for Keewaydin", is the question raised — and then only implicitly — as to what extent such an assumption is valid and, if it is valid, what are the problems involved in capturing life in poetry. Ondaatje is also often concerned here with the actual relationship between kinds of reality or modes of being. A handful of important poems deal explicitly with the relationship between the real and the oneiric, the conscious and the unconscious, and similarly related antithetical terms. The focus in these, however, is usually on the internal and external "dark" world, perceived only by the poem's speaker, which is shown variously as co-existent with the mundane, "Tink, the Summer Rider", vaguely threatening to it, "Gorillas", or in danger of being extirpated by it, "Dragon". "The Republic" is a representative and accessible early poem.

This house, exact,
coils with efficiency and style.
A different heaven here,
air even is remade in the basement.

The plants fed daily
stand like footmen by the windows,
flush with decent green
and meet the breeze with polish;
no dancing with the wind here.

Too much reason in its element:
passions crack the mask in dreams.
While we sleep
the plants in frenzy heave floors apart,
lust with common daisies,
feel rain,
fling their noble bodies, release a fart.
The clock alone, frigid and superior,
swaggers in the hall.

At dawn gardenias revitalize
and meet the morning with decorum.[4]

In the day this is a world of "reason" and order but at night the Dionysian world of primal vitality re-asserts itself and establishes the republic of the title. But the poem's point is that this world is there unperceived all the time. It is a necessary counter-balance to a world of "too much reason." The final couplet even suggests that its vitality and chaos "revitalize" the realm of order and light. It is typical of Ondaatje that the relationship between the two worlds is presented as a complex one and that no simplistic resolution is offered. Thus although "decorum" is restored at the poem's end, the verb "revitalize" serves as a disturbing reminder of the anarchic frenzy of the nighttime. The final couplet subtly reiterates the emotional tension created by the poem's central juxtaposition of two ostensibly opposed realities. This tension, as it relates to the theme, works against the formal closure arising inevitably with any poem's last word, and in doing so it implies a deliberate thematic irresolution which gives the poem the open-endedness characteristic of Ondaatje's best work.

While "The Republic" is primarily concerned with the description of a scene or an event, "Four Eyes" is more concerned with an examination of the actual process by which a poet transforms a lived, dynamic moment into poetry. The speaker, choosing to see only what is within his companion's field of vision, breaks from the moment in order to record it.

Naked I lie here
attempting to separate toes
with no help from hands.
You with scattered nightgown
listen to music, hug a knee.

I pick this moment up
with our common eyes
only choose what you can see

a photograph of you with posing dog
a picture with Chagall's red
a sprawling dress.

27

This moment I broke to record,
walking round the house
to look for paper.
Returning
I saw you, in your gaze,
still netted the picture, the dog.
The music continuing
you were still being unfurled
shaped by the scene.

I would freeze this moment
and in supreme patience
place pianos
and craggy black horses on a beach
and in immobilized time
attempt to reconstruct. (46)

In its focus on the act of creation the poem anticipates that group of difficult and ambitious lyrics in *Rat Jelly* all of which deal explicitly with this theme. "Four Eyes" does not examine the problem as perceptively as those more mature poems do but it nevertheless explores a similar area of creative experience. Ondaatje is concerned here with what happens when a poet tries to "reconstruct" a lived moment into art. In "Four Eyes" the first consequence of such an attempt is the poet's necessary separation from the experience itself. In order to write about it he must leave it: "This moment I broke to record." With its double meaning of separating and breaking, "broke" questions the quality of the writer's departure and suggests that ultimately he values art over life. Instead of being a participant he becomes a detached observer who prefers searching for a verbal equivalent of a lived moment to life itself. While "record" indicates the probability of a point by point imitation, the final stanza reveals that the reconstruction will be metaphoric. The writer will use "pianos/ and craggy black horses on a beach," images not present in the original scene. The poem ends by suggesting that the essential qualities of a scene "still being unfurled" can only be captured in metaphor. But Ondaatje's final lines simultaneously point to the possibility that even this reconstruction may misrepresent the original moment. The connotations of "freeze" and "immobilized time" imply that the poet will ultimately fail to do justice to life's temporal dimension and its dynamic quality. If my reading is correct then "Four Eyes" simultaneously offers a solution to the problem it poses, and a searching critique of that solution. It is not the best poem in Ondaatje's first volume — "Dragon" and "The Time Around Scars" are better — but together with "The Martinique" and "Eventually the Poem for Keewaydin" it is the one in which he most profoundly questions the possibilities of the kind of poetry he is writing.[5]

In his second book, the long narrative poem *the man with seven toes* (1969), the form and texture of the poem attempt to recreate for the reader the sense of an unpredictable and often chaotic experience "being unfurled" in the very body of the poem. Without resorting to formlessness Ondaatje nevertheless conveys the sense of a descent into a psychological and material chaos. The book is concerned with the response of an anonymous civilized woman (based on a 19th century Englishwoman, Mrs. Fraser) to a landscape and culture completely different from her own. Like Margaret Atwood's Susanna Moodie she is placed in a world whose reality is ostensibly unrelated to hers. The poem is the account of the confrontation with and gradual acceptance of the darker and more chaotic aspects of life which by the book's end are recognized as not only outside the self but within it as well.

Each of the brief self-contained lyrics vividly re-enacts a stage in her development.

goats black goats, balls bushed in the centre
cocks rising like birds flying to you reeling on you
and smiles smiles as they ruffle you open
spill you down, jump and spill over you
white leaping like fountains in your hair
your head and mouth till it dries
and tightens your face like a scar

Then up to cook a fox or whatever
goats eating goats heaving the bodies
open like purple cunts under ribs, then tear
like to you a knife down their pit, a hand in the warm
the hot the dark boiling belly and rip
open and blood spraying out like dynamite
caught in the children's mouths on the ground
laughing collecting it in their hands
or off to a pan, holding blood like gold
and the men rip flesh tearing, the muscles
nerves green and red still jumping
stringing them out, like you[6]

The syntax, imagery and rhythms, the very texture of the
verse, re-enact her complex response to an experience
which prior to becoming lost she had not even imagined.
The violent rape evokes a curiously ambivalent response;
some of the similes — "like birds," "white leaping like
fountains" — have quite positive connotations but their
hint of beauty suddenly disappears in an image — "a scar"
— which begins the comparison of the rape and the cutting
up of a fox. Her confusion and terror are brilliantly caught
in a simile which because of the deliberate absence of
punctuation has a double reference: "open and blood
spraying out like dynamite/ caught in the children's mouth
on the ground." Because of the syntactical ambiguity both
the blood and the dynamite are "caught in the children's
mouths"; this association of violence, sexuality and
innocence stunningly registers the woman's own shocked
response. But the similes in this lyric also fulfill another
function: they indicate her attempt to appropriate in terms
of analogous or more familiar images certain experiences
which she finds almost indescribably. In describing the
tearing apart of a fox in terms of rape, for example, she is
able to articulate her reaction to what has happened to
herself as well.

Yet despite her sufferings throughout the journey — and
"goats   black goats" is a typical instance — she is
described at the end of the book as lying on a bed and

sensing herself like a map, then
lowering herself into her body. (41)

This suggests that an increased awareness of herself has been gained from her experiences. The poem continues with the following stanzas:

In the morning she found pieces of a bird
chopped and scattered by the fan
blood sprayed onto the mosquito net,
its body leaving paths on the walls
like red snails that drifted down in lumps.

She could imagine the feathers
while she had slept
falling around her
like slow rain.

The violent death of the bird is a clear reminder of the world from which she had recently escaped. Her change in attitude to that world, however, is indicated in her ability to imagine the death of the birds in terms of "feathers/while she had slept/falling around her." Again like Atwood's Moodie she has achieved a new awareness of herself and of aspects of reality of which she had been previously ignorant.

A similar but even more developed and complex re-perception of reality takes place in *The Collected Works of Billy the Kid* (1970) whose events are consistently ambiguous in their significance, and whose central characters are both paradoxes. Billy the Kid is a murderer and "the pink of politeness/and as courteous a little gentleman/as I ever met."[7] Pat Garrett, the ostensible representative of law and order, is a "sane assassin sane assassin sane assassin sane assassin sane assassin" (29) with the final stress falling on "-in sane." In the world of *The Collected Works of Billy the Kid* peace and violence, sanity and insanity, order and chaos, and darkness and light are almost inextricably confused. It is as if the key characters have all made "the one altered move" (41) to

31

remove themselves from the normal expectations and moral judgements taken for granted by the reader.

Ondaatje's handling of the story subjects the reader to a process of defamiliarization in which the standard western made familiar by Burns, Borges, Penn and Peckinpah is deliberately "made new." Every aspect of Ondaatje's version emphasizes both the difficulties inherent in the attempt to perceive any complex, multifaceted reality and the artistic problems involved in recreating that reality in art. As in *the man with seven toes* Ondaatje achieves this by making the reader experience many of the episodes as if he were a direct witness to them, a temporary insider in the events themselves. But then in his normal position as an objective reader, inevitably outside the text, he must also stand back, organize and evaluate these "collected" but still, so to speak, disorganized "works" told from a variety of viewpoints and lacking a summarizing judgement by an omniscient narrator. The effect is similar to that achieved in Robbe-Grillet's fiction where the reader also enters a confusing fictive world knowing that there will be no ostensible authorial guidance. Both authors compel the reader to become both a surrogate character and a surrogate author in order to make him implicitly aware of the difficulties involved in the perceiving, organizing and describing of reality. The initial disorientation leads ultimately to a new awareness.

The allusions to Billy's non-picture (5), and the episodes which emphasize that the apparent is not the real serve a similar function. John Chisum's story of Livingstone, the mad breeder of dogs, is a case in point. Chisum says that Livingstone "seemed a pretty sane guy to me. I mean he didn't twitch or nothing like that" (60). This "pretty sane guy" "clinically and scientifically" (61) bred a race of mad dogs on his farm. Sallie Chisum reacts to the story by telling her bassett Henry, "Aint that a nasty story Henry, aint it? Aint it nasty." (62). The story may be "nasty" but its significance is not summed up in that judgement. The story is a reminder that we should refrain from assuming that the apparent is the real. If Livingstone was able to deceive John Chisum about his sanity then what kind of final judgement can the reader make about the sanity or insanity of Billy the Kid or Pat Garrett. Ondaatje's point is that the task of art is to present the reader with the "collected works" so that he can experience them in their total complexity. Thus Sally Chisum's final judgement of Billy and Pat, although more sympathetic toward Garrett than the book as a whole is, seems authoritative because it preserves their ambiguities and contradictions:

I knew both these men intimately.
There was good mixed in with the bad
in Billy the Kid
and bad mixed in with the good
in Pat Garrett.

No matter what they did in the world
or what the world thought of them
they were my friends.
Both were worth knowing. (89)

Despite Billy's death the book remains thematically open-ended. One of its last prose pieces suggests that Billy's story will be written again, interpreted again:

Imagine if you dug him up and brought him out. You'd see very little. There'd be the buck teeth. Perhaps Garrett's bullet no longer in thick wet flesh would roll in the skull like a marble. From the head there'd be a trail of vertebrae like a row of pearl buttons off a rich coat down to the pelvis. The arms would be cramped on the edge of what was the box. And a pair of handcuffs holding ridiculously fine ankle bones. (Even though dead they buried him in leg-irons). There would be the silver from the toe of each boot.

His legend a jungle sleep. (97)

The metaphor in the last line is almost oxymoronic and contains within itself both peace and a potential violence, Billy's gentleness and his killing. The image has an

33

undefined but thoroughly disturbing and haunting quality which leaves the reader with a sense of anticipation and even anxiety. It is as if the violence in Billy and the story is only temporarily quiescent. Ondaatje has managed to summarize within a single sensuous complex the unresolved tensions and ambiguities of the book.

While Ondaatje was writing his two longer works he was also working on those poems in *Rat Jelly* which as a group constitute his most explicit exploration of the relationship between poetry and reality: "King Kong meets Wallace Stevens," "Spider Blues," "Taking," "'the gate in his head'," "Burning Hills," and "White Dwarfs." In its concern with the creative mind's "fencing" of chaos the first of these is representative of the group.

Take two photographs—
Wallace Stevens and King Kong
(Is it significant that I eat bananas as I write this?)

Stevens is portly, benign, a white brush cut
striped tie. Businessman but
for the dark thick hands, the naked brain
the thought in him.

Kong is staggering
lost in New York streets again
a spawn of annoyed cars at his toes.
The mind is nowhere.
Fingers are plastic, electric under the skin.
He's at the call of Metro-Goldwyn-Mayer.

Meanwhile W.S. in his suit
is thinking chaos is thinking fences.
In his head the seeds of fresh pain
his exorcising,
the bellow of locked blood.

The hands drain from his jacket,
pose in the murderer's shadow.[8] (61)

The poem is structured upon a series of antitheses; the primary contrast is between Stevens, the businessman whose "thought is in him," and Kong whose "mind is nowhere." But as so often in Ondaatje's poetry the opposed terms are ultimately related. Kong, after all, is more than just a suggestive photographer's image of directable energy; he is also, as the poem's structure and imagery suggest, an aspect of Stevens himself, and the meeting between them occurs not only in the juxtaposing of their photographs but also within Stevens's mind. This is established by the presentation of analogous situations in the third and fourth stanzas: MGM directs Kong, Stevens fences the chaos and blood within himself. No comma or conjunction appear between the two clauses of "is thinking chaos is thinking fences" because the poem is suggesting the problematic simultaneity of both the "chaos" and the "fences" in the "thinking" of Stevens. If, as I have suggested, Kong and "chaos" or "blood" are synonomous then the entire fourth stanza points to Kong's presence within Stevens himself: both the containing form and the contained energy are within the mind of the businessman who is also a poet. This connection between the two is also present in the image of Stevens's "dark thick hands" which at the poem's end "drain from his jacket/pose in the murderer's shadow." The poem closes on the alarming association between Stevens and "the murderer's shadow" which can only be his own. He is a murderer because he has subdued his "chaos" or "blood," his unconscious self.[9]

But the poem also suggests, almost too casually, that Stevens is not the only poet with a shadow self. After all, the poem's writer-speaker asked humourously in the opening stanza "(Is it significant that I eat bananas as I write this?)" In view of the almost symbiotic relationship between Stevens and Kong there can only be one answer. Despite the parenthetical nature of the question, the image of the "bananas" functions as a comic allusion to the speaker's Kong-like aspect. Thus the poem indicates that both of the poets within it are in creative contact with everything that the ostensibly antithetical Kong represents; but they are able to transform, control and shape this "chaos" within the self into an aesthetic construct, into "King Kong meets Wallace Stevens." There is also a lingering suggestion, however, that some of the "chaos" will resist and even escape the poet's act of transformation. Both "the *bellow* of locked blood" and "hands *drain* from his jacket" (my italics) raise this possibility.[10]

The notion that the poet pays a price for creating a poem — "In his head the seeds of fresh pain/his exorcising" — reappears in "Spider Blues" in which the poet is seen as an admirable, because dextrous, spider.

I admire the spider, his control classic,
his eight legs finicky,
making lines out of the juice in his abdomen.
A kind of writer I suppose.
He thinks a path and travels
the emptiness that was there
leaves his bridge behind
looking back saying Jeez
did I do that?
and uses his ending
to swivel to new regions
where the raw of feelings exist. (63-64)

The spider as creative artist is a cartographer of the unknown and as the image in the last line reveals he brings back a message about some essential or primal reality. But like the speaker in "Four Eyes" he can only do this by separating himself from that reality. The spider may be more talented than the fly, yet in terms of the poem's allegory the fly, because it is closer to life, is the necessary subject matter of art.

And spider comes to fly, says
Love me I can kill you, love me
my intelligence has run rings about you
love me, I kill you for that clarity that
comes when roads I make are being made
love me, antisocial, lovely
* * * * * * * * * * * * * * * * * * * *

And the spider in his loathing
crucifies his victims in his spit
making them the art he cannot be.

Mind distinguishes Wallace Stevens from King Kong, "intelligence" the spider from the fly; but the cost of the distinction is registered by the poem's title, "Spider Blues": it is sung by Ray Charles or B.B. King, not Anne Murray.

But the poem is also a blues song because in the relationship between the spider and the fly, the former creates "beauty" by "crucifying" the latter. It is not clear what alternative modes of creation are possible but the suggestion is nevertheless felt that this is not an ideal relationship between art and life. If a poem is a mediation between mind and experience then the ultimate poem for Ondaatje is the one which transforms reality into poetry without "crucifying" it. "'the gate in his head'" is not that poem but it is Ondaatje's most emphatically pragmatic statement about what poetry should be.

My mind is pouring chaos
in nets onto the page.
A blind lover, dont know
what I love till I write it out.
And then from Gibson's your letter
with a blurred photograph of a gull.
Caught vision. The stunning white bird
an unclear stir.

And that is all this writing should be then.
The beautiful formed things caught at the wrong moment
so they are shapeless, awkward
moving to the clear. (62)

The "chaos" here is synonymous with whatever reality the poet has chosen to describe. It is the basic life stuff or substance out of which he shapes a poem. The poem's central tension is between this "chaos" and the mental "nets" of language within which the poet represents it. The "nets" recall the "fences" in "King Kong meets Wallace

37

Stevens", and the "webs" in "Spider Blues" and *The Collected Works of Billy the Kid*:[11] they are the actual medium — film or words — in which the vision is recreated or caught. Although "caught" is Ondaatje's word it doesn't really do justice to either his essentially heuristic assumption about poetic creativity — "A blind lover, dont know/what I love till I write it out," — nor to his concern with registering as sensitively as possible the dynamic quality of a moment or of an image. His concern is that the poem describe "the unclear stir" made by "a beautiful formed thing" perceived "at the wrong moment." This last detail is particularly important if the poetic perception is to yield a new, unexpected awareness of the image and, consequently, of reality. Yet as I pointed out earlier, the poem must deal with motion, flux and formlessness within the confines of poetic form. Ondaatje's poem achieves this by hinting at forms — the page, the photograph — and then subtly, through oxymoron, syntax and an interweaving of sounds — n's and r's — recreating the reality, the image of the bird.

The photograph is by Victor Coleman and the entire poem is a *hommage* to a writer whose extremely difficult poems reveal

> . . . the faint scars
> coloured strata of the brain,
> not clarity but *the sense of shift*. (my italics)

The "faint scars" are metaphors for Coleman's poems (*One Eye Love, Stranger*) which in a mode much more radical than Ondaatje's attempt to give the reader a sense of life as pure process, as "shift" and "chaos."[12] But the "scars" are also literally scars. Here, as elsewhere in Ondaatje's work, a physical scar represents caught motion, just as a mental scar or an emotional scar is caught memory.[13] In other words the scar literally incorporates and memorializes an emotion, an act or an experience. In terms of the imagery of "The Time Around Scars" a scar is a "medallion" or "watch" which records a violent and revealing event. One could even say that a scar is finally

38

analogous to an ideal, because non-verbal, poem in which the distinction between word and thing or state of being has finally disappeared. I shall return to this idea when discussing "White Dwarfs."

The very fact that in comparing his work to Coleman's Ondaatje writes "that is all this writing *should be* then" (my italics) is a reminder of an ideal which he feels he has not yet achieved. I would suggest that it is a mark of Ondaatje's integrity as a poet that his most successful poems raise this kind of question. He has said in an interview that "in writing you have to get all the truth down — the qualifications, the lies, the uncertainties —."[14] And if "'the gate in his head'" voices his doubts about the possibility — or impossibility — of an adequate linguistic representation — "all the truths" — of external or objective reality, "Burning Hills," one of his finest personal poems, indicates an awareness that any attempt to come to terms with an emotionally charged complex of memories carries with it its own difficulties.

Since he began burning hills
the Shell strip has taken effect.
A wasp is crawling on the floor
tumbling over, its motor fanatic.
He has smoked five cigarettes.
He has written slowly and carefully
With great love and great coldness.
When he finishes he will go back
hunting for the lies that are obvious.

(*Rat Jelly*, p.58)

Unlike most of Ondaatje's personal poems this one is written, almost over-insistently (He has .../ He has"), in the third person. The repetition of the pronoun suggests the attempted, and not completely realized, distancing of his personal memories. The "burning hills," the wasp and the five cigarettes are not random details; their cumulative significance is to point to how difficult it is for him to achieve an attitude of "great love and great coldness." Yet this is how he must write in order to achieve a successful,

39

because objective, recreation of his personal experiences. In his poem his "coldness," both emotional and tonal, is evident in the ending's unsentimental and deliberately monotoned voice "hunting for the lies that are obvious." In what sounds like a line from Cohen's *The Energy of Slaves* (but isn't) Ondaatje is indicating that despite his attempts at objectivity his poem may be a misrepresentation or lie. And if the lies to be sought out are the "obvious" ones there is the disturbing implication that the "un-obvious" lies will remain. In either case, the reader has been warned about the poem and the poet's limitations in getting "all the truth down."

Ondaatje's most radical gesture in the direction of indicating that there are times when "all the truth" cannot be stated, described or re-enacted is the final poem in *Rat Jelly*, "White Dwarfs." Here the poet confronts not just the unconscious, or process, or chaos, but events that in their total human significance seem to demand a response of awed silence. A variation of T.W. Adorno's "No poetry after Auschwitz,"[15] the poem is a profound meditation on both life and art. It is a tribute to those who have gone beyond "social fuel" and language.

This is for those people who disappear
for those who descend into the code
and make their room a fridge for Superman
— who exhaust costume and bones that could perform
                                                    flight,
who shave their moral so raw
they can tear themselves through the eye of a needle
this is for those people
that hover and hover
and die in the ether peripheries. (70)

The key word here is "moral" which although slightly ambiguous does seem to be synonymous with "life-meaning" or mode of being. Those who "shave their moral . . . raw" live in a condition in which their character or self exists without a social persona, "where there is no social fuel"; consequently they come in touch with the very

40

ground of their being which is here quite subtly associated with heaven ("through the eye of a needle").[16] Like Ondaatje's outlaws (Billy), alienated loners (Pat Garrett and Charlie Wilson), and sufferers (Philoctetes, his father) they are the ones who can provide a glimpse of what the terrifyingly brilliant poem about his father calls the "other worlds"[17] lying beyond either consciousness or social forms.

In "White Dwarfs" the speaker admires those people whose achievement or experience in patience or suffering is beyond him.

Why do I love most
among my heroes those
who sail to that perfect edge
where there is no social fuel
Release of sandbags
to understand their altitude—

That silence of the third cross
3rd man hung so high and lonely
we dont hear him say
say his pain, say his unbrotherhood
What has he to do with the smell of ladies
can they eat off his skeleton of pain?

Himself afraid of "no words of/falling without words" he loves those whose language is an expressive and deafening silence: for them the experience and their expression of it are one. Silence is here a final poetry — like the earlier image of a scar — which cannot be improved upon by the poet's facility with words. This is a supreme fiction in which the dualities of nets and chaos, Wallace Stevens and King Kong, art and life, words and objects have been finally dissolved but only at a price which the traditional poet cannot pay. Even as he suggests that poetry in such a context would be superfluous and perhaps blasphemous he is nevertheless writing a poem. Like other poets who interrogate the validity of language — Rozewicz and Celan, for example — Ondaatje inevitably uses language to conduct that interrogation.[18] This dialectic of language and silence leads finally not to despair about poetry but to an affirmation. The confirmation with a reality which at first seemed resistant to the "nets" of verbal representation has not silenced the poet, rather it has provoked him into an even more ambitious poetry. In the poem's final movement he attempts to describe the unknown.

And Dashiell Hammet in success
suffered conversation and moved
to the perfect white between words

This white that can grow
is fridge, bed,
is an egg — most beautiful
when unbroken, where
what we cannot see is growing
in all the colours we cannot see

there are those burned out stars
who implode into silence
after parading in the sky
after such choreography what would they wish to speak
                                        of anyway (71)

The poem ends by pointing hauntingly to a beauty ("an egg") and a human profundity (the personified "star") which are beyond more explicit description and discussion. The poem's tentative metaphoric gestures are all that can be expected of poetry in such a situation. Yet Ondaatje's willingness to risk these inevitably anti-climactic lines ("after such choreography"), to explore "the perfect white between words" and "the colours we cannot see," is a paradoxical attestation of his belief in poetry.

Dashiell Hammett's unexplained retreat away from life and art into "the perfect white between words" anticipates the events of *Coming Through Slaughter* (1976)[19] which deals with the life of the legendary jazz cornetist Charles

Buddy Bolden (1876-1931). Ondaatje uses Bolden's life, which like Mrs. Fraser's and Billy the Kid's, occurred, for the most part, "away from recorded history," as the basis of a novel developing the ideas about art introduced in his earlier work. The dust-jacket is correct when it suggests that this is ultimately a novel about the very nature of the creative process, Ondaatje's as well as Bolden's. Because it is his most extended treatment of the very nature of a certain kind of creativity, the novel needs to be discussed at greater length than any of the earlier works.

In *Coming Through Slaughter*, as in the two longer works, history and facts "have been expanded and polished to suit the truth of fiction" (Ondaatje's end-note). Paradoxically, the facts by themselves — the photograph, the interviews, the gossip — are almost meaningless in that they give only a superficial explanation of Bolden's life. Only through the necessary complement of Ondaatje's "truth of fiction" can this particular history take on meaning. But it would be a misunderstanding of both Ondaatje's view of art and his vision of life to see him as postulating the possibility of a single unambiguous meaning. For the reader, as for the detective Webb, facts and stories about Buddy's life are "like spokes on a rimless wheel ending in air" (63). The simile captures perfectly the reader's own sense of the ambiguity and the indefiniteness of Bolden's life. The various stories about Bolden, both history's and Ondaatje's, suggest possibilities, meanings rather than any final single view.

Ondaatje's central character is a man who attempts to lead in both his daily life and in his music a life of complete spontaneity: "He did nothing but leap into the mass of changes and explore them and all the tiny facets so that eventually he was almost governed by fears of certainty" (15). His loud spontaneous music is a perfect mirror or embodiment of his mode of being, and is similar to the ideal poetry Ondaatje described in "'the gate in his head'"; and like the blurred photograph of Ondaatje on the back cover, the music communicates "the sense of shift" that is reality itself.[20] Frank Lewis's description of Bolden's music makes this explicit:

He tore apart the plot — see his music was immediately on top of his own life. Echoing. As, when he was playing he was lost and hunting for the right accidental notes. Listening to him was like talking to Coleman. You were both changing direction with every sentence, sometimes in the middle, using each other as a springboard through the dark. You were moving so fast it was unimportant to finish and clear everything. He would be describing something in 27 different ways. There was pain and gentleness everything jammed into each number. (37)

Bolden's newspaper, *The Cricket*, also reflects this obsession with the partial, the immediate, the transient:

The Cricket existed between 1899 and 1905. It took in and published all the information Bolden could find. It respected stray facts, manic theories, and well-told lies. This information came from customers in the chair and from spiders among the whores and police that Bolden and his friends knew. *The Cricket* studied broken marriages, gossip about jazzmen and a servant's memoirs told everyone that a certain politician spent twenty minutes each morning deciding which shirt to wear. Bolden took all the thick facts and dropped them into his pail of sub-history. (24)

But the key to understanding Bolden's character lies in relationship to his wife Nora Bast in whom he finds the certainties and patterns he both "loathed and needed" (78):

He distrusted [certainty] in anyone but Nora for there it went to the spine, and yet he attacked it again and again in her, cruelly, hating it, the sure lanes of the probable. Breaking chairs and windows glass doors in fury at her certain answers. (15-16)

Despite his ostensible rejection of certainties and patterns in his life Bolden needs, even craves, Nora's stabilizing,

44

almost normalizing, influence to save him from being overwhelmed by the chaos he embraces whenever he becomes Buddy Bolden the public figure and musician. This irreconcilable tension between two contradictory needs within Bolden becomes exacerbated when he begins to realize that even his musical career — as opposed to his music — is a trap, a predictable pattern of events: everyone expects Buddy Bolden to be exciting, spontaneous, predictably unpredictable. As Bolden puts it much later,

All my life I seemed to be a parcel on a bus. I am the famous fucker. I am the famous barber. I am the famous cornet player. Read the labels. . . . (106)

Bolden's desire to escape this situation is prompted by his contact with another artist, Bellocq, the diminutive photographer of the whores of New Orleans. As Bolden realizes, Bellocq tempted him "out of the world of audiences where I had tried to catch everything thrown at me" (91). Bellocq is also an artist but unlike Bolden he attempts to capture reality solely for his own pleasure. A man who does not "rely on anything" he offers Bolden "the black empty spaces" of a completely private existence away from art and, finally, even away from life itself. The scene in which Bellocq develops the photograph of Frank Lewis's band underscores this crucial point:

[Webb and Bellocq] watching the pink rectangle as it slowly began to grow black shapes, coming fast now. Then the sudden vertical lines which rose out of the pregnant white paper which were the outlines of the six men and their formally held instruments. . . . All serious except for the smile on Bolden. Watching their friend float into the page smiling at them, the friend who in reality had reversed the process and gone back into white, who in this bad film seemed to have already half-receded with that smile which may not have been a smile at all, which may have been his mad dignity. (52-53)

During his two year escape into this "white" Bolden sheds his reputation, and rediscovers both himself and the basics of his music. But as Ondaatje subtly indicates in a sensuously lyrical scene, for an artist like Bolden there can never be any final escape from the inner compulsions driving him towards his art. As Buddy talks to and touches Jaelin she realizes

> that while they spoke his fingers had been pressing the flesh on her back as though he were plunging them into a cornet. She was sure he was quite unaware, she was sure his mind would not even remember. It was part of a conversation held with himself in his sleep. Even now as she lay against his body in her red sweater and skirt. But she was wrong. He had been improving on *Cakewalking Babies*. (57)

Buddy has only one choice, to play, to create as intensely as possible until he breaks.

When Bolden finally returns to New Orleans he attempts to play during a parade the impossible music he had discovered during his escape into silence. In a finely paced climactic scene Bolden is provoked by a woman dancing sensuously in perfect rhythm with his music. He begins to play just for her until his notes and her body (art and life) become indistinguishable, until, in a startling reversal, her dance compels him to go further than he seems to have intended. Unable to sustain the intensity of this kind of ultimate music he collapses into a twenty-four year silence. Ironically it is a madness within which he finds a perfect contentment now that the tensions within him have been finally resolved. Even as he is collapsing Bolden is thinking, "this is what I wanted, always, the loss of privacy in the playing" (130). But "this is what I wanted" is ambiguous because it also refers to the madness which assures him the silence and the privacy he craved beyond art.

As I suggested earlier *Coming Through Slaughter* is ultimately about the nature of the creative process — Bolden's, Bellocq's, Audobon's[21] and Ondaatje's — and its most provocative suggestion is that in certain artists creativity and self-destruction — Bellocq's "making and destroying" (55) — are of necessity almost co-extensive. To a generation that has witnessed the suicides of Borowski, Celan, Plath and Berryman the idea in itself is hardly startling but what is remarkable is Ondaatje's sensitive exploration of how the tensions within a particular kind of artist can only be resolved by being transmuted into art (*Coming Through Slaughter* or music) or madness. I equate Ondaatje's novel and Bolden's music because Ondaatje suggests a resemblance between himself and the jazz musician. In one of the novel's most surprising and haunting passages he treats Bolden as a mirror image of himself:

When I read he stood in front of mirrors and attacked himself, there was the shock of memory. For I had done that. Stood, and with a razorblade cut into cheeks and forehead, shaved hair. Defiling people we did not wish to be. . . .

The thin sheaf of information. Why did my senses stop at you? There was the sentence, "Buddy Bolden who became a legend when he went berserk in a parade . . .' What was there in that, before I knew your nation your colour your age, that made me push my arm forward and spill it through the front of your mirror and clutch myself? (133–34)

It is apparent from the overall context that Ondaatje admires Bolden because the latter is an artist who has gone, for whatever reason, too far in his commitment to a demanding art. His sensibility was so compulsively responsive to the pressure of life's dynamism and confusion that in order to represent its complexities he took risks with his own sanity. In attempting to articulate aspects of this reality (both internal and external) Bolden went mad: "his mind on the pinnacle of something collapsed" (133). That evasively understated "something" points to an ultimate art, a negation of our more conservative and less daring notions of art, which is paradoxically almost indistinguishable from the reality within which it originates, and with which the artist has merged in order to produce it. It involves a projection of self so extreme — "his music was immediately on top of his own life" (37) — that the result is a total loss of self whether through madness or suicide. In the light of this the inescapable suggestion evoked by Ondaatje's comparing of himself to Bolden is that for now, in this work, he has succeeded in evading a fate somehow analogous to Bolden's.

If as the novel's last sentence states, "There are no prices" (156) for this kind of life or art, the novel also attests that there can be no simple explanations offered either. Despite the facts, statistics, interviews, fictions, and various viewpoints offered Bolden's life remains enigmatic, his compulsive talent unexplained. The best that Ondaatje's art can do is to recreate as sensitively as possible the lived texture of this dynamic and ultimately inexplicable reality. Where his earlier work was content, for the most part, simply to indicate the more formal problems involved in such a recreation, his latest and most brilliant book goes one necessary step further and explores the frightening personal implications of his view of art.

Such an attitude certainly confirms Sheila Watson's contention that Ondaatje is both "intelligent" ("as intelligent as Auden") and not "afraid of what living means."[23] To be unafraid of life involves a willingness to confront and, if one is an artist, to describe reality in its full complexity. Ondaatje's work is the result of such repeated confrontations.

[1] Michael Onddatje, *Rat Jelly*, Toronto: Coach House Press, 963, p. 62.

[2] The comparison with Stevens, who appears in two of Onaatje's poems, is obvious and could be developed.

[3] R.P. Blackmur, *Form and Value in Modern Poetry*, New York: Anchor, 1957, p. 23.

[4] Michael Ondaatje, *The Dainty Monsters*, Toronto: Coach House Press, 1967, p. 20.

[5] This self-questioning about aesthetic issues becomes gradually more explicit until it becomes the central theme of a group of poems in *Rat Jelly*.

[6] Michael Ondaatje, *The Collected Works of Billy the Kid*, Toronto: House of Anansi, 1970, p. 87.

[8] Cf. "King Kong" in which Kong represents an aspect of the self, "we renew him/capable in the zoo of night" p. 44.

[9] Cf. "Heron Rex" in *Rat Jelly*, p. 52.

[10] Cf. Atwood's "The green man": "They did not look/in his green pockets, where he kept/his hands changing their shape". *The Animals in that Country*, Toronto: Oxford University Press, 1968, p. 13.

[11] Billy describes the cobwebs in a barn as follows: "When I walked in I avoided the cobwebs who had places to grow to, who had stories to finish. The flies caught in those acrobat nets were the only murder I saw" (*The Collected Works of Billy the Kid*, p. 17). For a slightly different use of this imagery of webs and acrobats see the beautifully restrained lyric "We're at the graveyard" in *Rat Jelly*, p. 51. See also the detective Webb, and the spies or "spiders" in *Coming Through Slaughter* (24).

[12] For the source of Ondaatje's title see *One Eye Love*, Toronto: Coach House Press, 1967, "Day 20".

[13] Leonard Cohen, *The Favourite Game*, Toronto: McClelland and Stewart, 1970, p. 8.

[14] *Rune*, Spring 1975, Number 2, p. 50.

[15] T.W. Adorno, "Engagement," in *Noten zur Literatur III* (Frankfurt amm Main: Suhrkamp Verlag, 1965), pp. 125-6.

[16] For other (and rare) examples of Ondaatje's unobtrusive use of traditional images and symbols see the apple in "Burning Hill" (*Rat Jelly*, p. 58), and the pearls in "Henri Rousseau and Friends" (*The Dainty Monsters*, p. 26).

[17] *Rat Jelly*, p. 24.

[18] For a detailed examination of the whole notion of a self-questioning literature and of a literature of silence see Susan Sontag's *Styles of Radical Will*, New York: Delta Books, 1967 *passim*.

[19] *Coming Through Slaughter*, Toronto: House of Anansi, 1976. All references will be to this text.

[20] Compare bpNichol in *the martyrology*, book II, Toronto: Coach House Press, 1972: "ah reason/there is only feeling/knowing the words are/i am/this moment is/everything present and tense/i write despite my own misgivings/say things as they do occur/the mind moves truly/is it free."

[21] Audobon is mentioned at least twice. The first time is during a dialogue between Bolden and Nora's mother about Audobon's drawings of what she claims are "psychologically neurotic creatures" (25). The second direct reference occurs in the novel's penultimate paragraph and reminds the reader that on his way to the asylum Bolden passes through the country in which Audobon did his drawing. The point of these references and other allusions in the text seems to be that Bolden is — the metaphor is inescapable — a strange "bird".

[22] "there is no beauty in madness." bpNichol, *the martyrology*, book I, Toronto: Coach House Press, 1972.

[23] "Michael Ondaatje: The Mechanization of Death," *Open Letter*, Third Series, No. I (Winter 1974-5), p. 161.

'Local Poet Deserves Attention': The Poetics of David McFadden

Ronald Kiverago

The ever increasing number of Canadian poetry publications is by now a well documented fact. George Woodcock in his editorial essay 'Swarming of Poets',[1] outlines the difficulties that this fact creates for editors and reviewers alike. On the other hand, the career of David McFadden presents a good example of a corresponding difficulty encountered by the Canadian writer. To date, he has six major book-length publications that have aroused the interest of reviewers less than twenty times.

The Poem Poem,[2] McFadden's first book, is an example of his work that has received almost no critical attention. This neglect is particularly important because this book exhibits and describes poetic techniques that are used throughout his subsequent work. *The Poem Poem* is about the writing of poems. It uses as its central metaphor an equation of the gestation period of the human child to the 'gestation' of a poem. The beginning of the creative process is a private event; inspiration and subsequent linguistic construction are complex organic processes.

a flower / inside me

```
        the cellular growth
of the poem. unseen
              point of beginning

flower / union of complex desires
```
                                        (*The Poem Poem*, p. 4)

McFadden states that, as in the conception of the child, the germination of the smallest particle is the actual beginning-place of what is to become the physical object. However, as growth toward a larger physical reality takes place, McFadden observes that it is the special quality possessed by each of the individual internal parts that is of importance to the nature of the finished object; and that the perfection of the resulting creation depends upon the relationship that is established between each part and its complementary. What this means in terms of the poem, McFadden is saying, is that each part, such as syllable, line and image, is important in contributing not only to the wholeness of the poem but also to its perfection.

```
the perfect length of a perfect poem

taking syllables into account
and its complementary

each image
its associative

poem of unravelling
bird-geneology

'The Perfect Universe'
```
                                        (*The Poem Poem*, p. 7)

The stress given by McFadden to the fact that the poem, like the child, starts inside the body and his emphasis upon the internal parts of a poem, their relation to each other and their ultimate creation of a physical object outside the body on the page, is a statement of his poetic theory not only on inspiration, the creative process, but also on the necessity that the poem be regarded as an object of reality.

In order that he might be better equipped to receive poetic stimuli — so that his body may become a 'library' — McFadden declares that he must 'keep good & empty' of preconceived notions such as 'In Labor — Expect the Worst'. To achieve a state of greater awareness, he is saying, is to allow the body the possibility of inspiration. McFadden employs a collage of radio reports, newspaper reports, unrelated quotations and prose passages that imply the number of alien forces at work that daily invade the poet's senses via the media. These sources of information, however, are not inspirational for it is only after they have ceased, when the poet begins to feel his bodily sensations again, that the poems begin.

Similarly, McFadden utilizes the device of capitalization of such terms as 'Death Wish' and 'Man' in order to convey their theoretical meanings, as opposed to the physical realities of 'death' and 'man'. He states that preoccupation with such theory is a useless endeavour and observes that it is when concern is focussed upon physical truth that poetic inspiration occurs. Poetry for McFadden is not didactic statement resulting from rational logic. Instead, poems spring from a multitude of bodily sensations that are so complex that 'The dream is simple, / transcends numbers'.

The only attention that has been devoted to *The Poem Poem* is a review article by Douglas Barbour.[3] This is unfortunate, because in this instance Barbour displays poor critical judgement and his literay analysis is unsubstantiated. Thus he fails to aid the potential reader whom he purports to serve. He condemns the book for its content, saying that its 'focus is only inwards'. The title of the book itself is sufficient to tell the reader what the poem is about, and even an initial perusal at the book-stand reveals that the focus of the book is concerned with bringing the poem *out* of the body and onto the page as a physical object of reality. Barbour claims that *The Poem Poem* is 'written under the influence of Williams' *Paterson* and Olson's *Maximus Poems*'. However, he fails to support this claim with literary evidence. His chief criticism is that he disliked the effect of McFadden's use of collage, and lost interest in the poem. This attitude offers no analysis of the literary device, and reflects merely the poetic tastes of the reviewer, rather than critical judgement of the effectiveness of the collage technique.

Collage is a technique used by McFadden frequently in his later work. In particular, the visual media of the photograph, in *Letters from the Earth to the Earth*, and the sketch drawing, in *The Great Canadian Sonnet*, are presented in collage with the written sight-sound medium of these works. The photographs in *Letters from the Earth to the Earth*[4] are not the issue of either artistic or professional-commercial camera work. Rather, they have the quality of the family snap-shot album about them, both in their photographic qualities and in their subject matter. The camera focus is sometimes blurred, (lower, opposite 'God, the'); most often the depth of field encompasses a welter of background / foreground detail that detracts attention from both the subject and the theme of the photograph (above 'Keys'); and there is ample evidence of over and under light exposure (upper, opposite 'David and Joan' and above 'Phases of the Moon', respectively) to indicate the approach of the amateur. The subject matter of friends and family at park gatherings and on holiday (above 'May I Listen to Me:') contributes to the album effect.

It would be misguided to assume that it was McFadden's intention to match the photographs to the poems of this book.[5] It is also wrong to assume that the lack of either an artistic or a professional quality represents a flaw in the effect that they produce. McFadden uses the photographs to fashion a background against which the poems are set, in much the same way that Robert Minden's photographs establish the locale and the nature of the inhabitants of Daphne Marlatt's *Steveston*.[6] The subject matter of McFadden's poems are his wife and children, his friends and those people and events around him who are engaged in the pursuits of everyday life.

> If I waited a few days I could make a real well-wrought
> > poem out
> of this, but hell this is my way.
> > ("An Hour's Restless Sleep")

His way is to observe and capture the moments of existence in the Twentieth Century. To make the poem 'well-wrought' would be false to his vision.

The Great Canadian Sonnet[7] used the line drawings of Greg Curnoe to underscore the message of the novel. These drawings present the images of a popular culture based on the radio and television advertisement media. Ricky Wayne, the poet-protagonist-narrator of the novel, states that he wants 'to come up with a really good poem' so that he might contribute 'to the story of the human race'. However, every attempt that he makes is side-tracked by the culture in which he lives. The drawings juxtapose the images of that culture against Wayne's literary attempts. He wants to accomplish a noble literary achievement but can only 'think of the money to be made if others like it' and it becomes a popular bestseller. As in *The Poem Poem*, the poet is subject to the consciousness-invading culture he lives in. Values based on popular merit, McFadden is saying, are destructive to literary achievement.

The line drawings are accompanied by captions that are taken from the written text of the novel. This technique produces an advertisement-type effect that emphasizes the commercial aspect of the cultural images that are being presented. The physical form of the novel is similar to the format of children's 'little-books' — a similarity that is emphasized by the cartoon-like quality of the line drawings. These two devices combine to under-cut the seriousness of the novel's title and thereby satirize the literary attempt implied by the title. The fact that the images of both the written and visual sections originate in a commercialized culture that is primarily American implies that under this influence the Canadian literary achievement is a branchplant product of the American way of life. By the use of these devices, McFadden not only expresses an anti-American comment but also makes a strong nationalistic statement about the need for a separate culture that is Canadian in origin.

McFadden's poetry, however, is rooted in this *kitsch* culture and presents a view of the common man striving to cope with the realities of his time.[8] One of the chief methods that the poetry uses to develop this theme is the family relationship. The special connection between family members is a concern of the poet in *Letters from the Earth to the Earth*.

> 'I study her face so carefully
> every day because she's changing so,'
> Says Joan, about the child
>
> My stomach moving slowly,
> April sunlight from the window
> touching Joan's face in ways
> I never saw before.

('Tick Talk')

The mother's awareness of the changing features of the child alters not only her own appearance but also the poet's perception of her. Other poems, such as 'The Fire Thief' and 'No Matter' chart the poet's observation of his children as their growing awareness reassembles the specific nature of their environment. In *Poems Worth Knowing*[9] the child's trial and error method of learning allows the poet to comment on the importance of differing perceptions in establishing matters such as good taste ('A Taste of Honey'). In this relationship even the consumer attitudes towards such things as 'Coke' and 'Diet-Cola' can be used as a means of measuring the poet's perception of his wife ('Journey to Love'). What McFadden is saying is that observation rooted in even the smallest and most insignificant aspects of human life are worthy of comment. He uses the naive learning processes of his family as a device that strips away his preconceived notions of the universe, thereby allowing a record to be made of the beauty and joy that exists even in the trivia of a *kitsch* culture.

Although the later poetry, represented by *Intense Pleasure* and *A Knight in Dried Plums*, makes less frequent reference to the family, McFadden continues to recognize the importance of the family relationship as a means for expression. *Intense Pleasure*[10] emphasises the importance of defining the family's identity in terms of its physical reality. A list of 'Exclusive Addresses' not only suggests the lower-middle-class urban locale of the family's origins but also stresses the necessity of accepting the characteristic implied by this specific setting in the physical universe. McFadden recognizes the myth-making force that tradition presents as well as his responsibility to take his proper place within that tradition ('T.S.Eliot');but he realizes that his past is an inseparable part of his present, and appreciates the impossibility of an existence based solely on tradition ('Titles I Have Heard but not Read'). McFadden's use of the family as a means to express these themes indicates his view that the roots that are needed to establish an identity are to be found in those aspects of man's life that are most intimate to him — such as the factual nature of his family history, and the relationships he has with the members of his family.

That the events shaping these relationships are based on a culture that has its orientation in popular tastes emphasises McFadden's acceptance of the realities of the culture as an important influence on man's life. McFadden uses factual statement as well as specific reference to this culture as a device to support this expression. For example, the point-blank statement 'A red dumptruck goes by with / T.A. DOWLING on its side' juxtaposes the ominous, irrevocable force of change against man's apathetic 'but it's too hot' ('When All This was Farm'). Extinction of man's natural environment, implied by a 'polluted shoreline', is the background against which are set the spectator attitudes of a society cynical of vandalism and concerned only with watching such things as a 'car rally' or an 'old English movie on Cinema Six' ('Polluted Shoreline'). *A Knight in Dried Plums*[11] uses this device to show the powerful attitude-shaping influence that the American television and cinema culture has on the

Canadian family. The family visiting America becomes so engrossed in this culture that they accept illusion for fact, and respond in a stereotyped manner:

In Washington we stopped to help a stranded motorist
& he was a French-Canadian scared we were
going to mug him & we did. That's all folks.
("A Typical Canadian Family Visits Disney World")

McFadden's use of specific reference to *kitsch* aspects of the culture in which he lives emphasises the importance of recognizing these elements as factors shaping the identity. His use of the direct statement implies observation based on physical objects, and, in juxtaposition with other statements, illustrates the threat these objects pose to the identity.

If values based on the *kitsch* tastes of a predominately alien culture play an important part in establishing man's identity, then differing senses of perception are necessary in order to prevent a loss of identity. *Intense Pleasure* has several poems devoted to this theme. McFadden utilizes the devices of direct statement and a form of it, the multiple poem, to express aspects of perception. For example, the feelings aroused by a post card from Bermuda ('A Picture of Bermuda') are juxtaposed on the same page against the domestic complaints about the unpleasant physical sensations of a dissatisfying breakfast ('Desert'). By the statement that:

The handwriting,
stamp & picture of Bermuda
will look funny 40 years from now.

it is implied that time has an important role in the way things are perceived. In retrospect, the events of the present seem trivial. Similarly, 'A True Poem', 'Correction' and 'Books' all appear on the same page and, in triple juxtaposition, offer an expression about perception. The first poem gives an interpretation of life, based on the bodily sensations and viewpoint of a six-year-old. The

58

correct statement of fact, in the second poem, contains insufficient information to be of any use and leaves questions unanswered by its lack of relative context. The last poem emphasises the isolating and distancing effect of formal structures such as 'hedge', 'houses' and 'books'. When taken together these three small poems give expression to the larger notion that the particular viewpoint relative to each individual is more important in the determination of truth than are formally structured, detached and unrelated facts. By use of the same device the difference between literal and figurative expression is made in 'Act of God', 'Popular Science' and 'After the Rain'. In each poem the statement of a literal truth is followed by figurative expression. Consider 'Popular Science':

Running my finger tips along
the belly of the sky

Red sun setting
beneath hydro wires.

The repetition of the juxtaposed literal and figurative values stresses the importance of perception in assessing truth. In all of these poems McFadden is concerned with the part that different viewpoints play in determining the perception of reality. By the use of factual statement juxtaposed within the multiple poem, the confusing nature of isolated truths is stressed; taken together the poems present a more homogeneous view of reality based on facts perceived in their relative contexts.

Although much of his poetry is centered on the local details and events of his home town, McFadden uses the journey as a device to broaden his perception of the society in which he lives. In *Intense Pleasure* a view is given of the effect of an alien culture on a man returning to his native Hamilton from a long journey ('Last Move'). The man is described as having refused help with his luggage despite the fact that he has more than he can easily manage by himself. In addition, he is dressed inadequately for the cold weather and is relying on public transportation to carry him and his baggage to their destination. Thus the highly individualistic personality of this man is established. However, the use of 'ah' and 'mah' for 'I' and 'my' in his speech indicates the cultural effect that his visit to Texas has had on his personality. His acknowledgement of this effect is contained in the closing lines:

> Ah went down there 6 years ago
> to see what all them draft dodgers were runnin' from
> & now I know.

McFadden is saying that American culture exerts such a powerful influence on Canadians that even the speech patterns of a highly individualistic person are affected. The final use of 'I' indicates that only by returning to the place of one's physical origins can one escape this influence.

A *Knight In Dried Plums* makes clear McFadden's position on the American way of life.

> The U.S. tourists who remain here
> are the ones who bother me,
> the ones that are gradually filling
> more and more influential positions here
> & the ones that are buying up more & more
> Georgian Bay or Pacific Coast islands.

> I think they unconsciously want to start
> the whole damn experiment over again up here
> & I would rather starve than see that happen.
>
>   ('U.S. Tourists')

The American visitors are described in terms of stereotyped behaviour, such as their erratic and drunken driving, their illegal possession of firearms and the aggressive actions of their children. McFadden uses these stereotyped attitudes as devices by which he shows the view that Canadians have of U.S. tourists. Similarly, the American view of Canadians is expressed in 'Incident At Parrsboro'. The publicity-shunning attitudes of a well-known Canadian song-writer, Dick Elliott, are judged by an American tourist to be a method of income-tax evasion. The question, 'You got/ RCA Victor up here, haven't you?' indicates the stereotyped American view of Canada as being a culturally and technologically deprived wasteland.

The stereotyped view that Canadians have of Canada and of other Canadians is shown in 'Somewhere South of Springhill'. Springhill is described as a one-time mine disaster town, complete with an almost-victim of the disaster who has his own personal story to tell. As well, there is a local celebrity, Anne Murray, who is seen embracing the principles of a quiet homey-life 'playing volleyball/ in the backyard with her brothers'. The personal almost-disaster that besets the poet and his family is prevented by the fraternal attentions of two brothers. Springhill is described as a peaceful small town that always has the air of disaster about it: once it was the mines and now it is the deer who create hazards by standing on the road.

These poems give several impressions of Canadian culture. By the use of the journey McFadden is able to collect information about his country from a broader area than he would have been able to in the local home town setting. The use of stereotyped attitudes is a device by which McFadden presents the superficial generalities of a culture based on popular tastes. All of these poems make use of the reportage techniques of simple prose-like verse that give a factual recounting of the events and details of the journey. This technique creates the effect of story-telling, an effect that supports the generalities expressed by the journey.

Another journey that the poet undertakes is that of the fantasy. McFadden uses the fantasy in *Intense Pleasure* as a device to express the nature of reality. For example, his turtle is initially defined in terms of the logical physical objects of her environment and her visible actions:

> 10-gallon aquarium
> filter, pump, landing platform,
> gravel, clear water
> splash, dive, glide, surface, float, slowly sink.

('Natalie')

However, in his fantasy the logic of physical objects does not apply and she 'becomes a softsweet 16-year-old virgin' who slips into his bed. Similarly, a system of proof based on logical, scientific methods establishes the fact of the poet's pregnancy, despite the biological impossibility and the fact 'This is all taking place in a hotel lobby' ('He Knew He Was Pregnant'). Also, the fear of physical paralysis is given expression by means of the fantasy creation of a witch's spell ('An Old Witch'). These poems use the fantasy as a device by which the logic of the rational world of objects is juxtaposed with the logic of the irrational world of the imagination. McFadden is saying in these poems that not only is it important to be able to perceive reality from a variety of viewpoints but also that it is necessary to understand the part that irrational forces of the mind play in determining what is normally considered to be truth based on rationally verifiable logic.

One of the effects of the fantasy device in *A Knight In Dried Plums* is that of wish fulfillment. 'The Spoiled Brat' expresses the narrator's dislike for a small child and uses the fantasy as a means to fulfil the wish to torture him. When the results of the fantasy are analyzed in terms of factual reality, the danger of the irrational is stressed:

                    ...the gun
    went off & he fell to the floor with
    half his head blown off.

When viewed strictly in terms of fantasy, however, the wish fulfillment produces a cathartic effect, relieving the desire to torture the small boy. The same sort of effect is produced by the fantasy in 'Death of a Man Who Owned A Swimming Pool'. In a similar way the actual enactment of the fantasy has dangerous results, while the fulfillment in terms of the fantasy relieves the narrator of his dislike of privately owned luxury.

Whereas these two poems illustrate the fantasy of wish fulfillment, other poems in *A Knight of Dried Plums* use the fantasy solely as a vehicle of self-expression. In other words, these fantasies have no ulterior motive other than the expression of the poet's thoughts. For example, the unreal nature of a child's deformities and his startling claim of kinship to the poet are statements indicating that 'Scar Tissue' is a fantasy that demonstrates the poet's compassionate feelings towards the physical suffering of fellow beings. Similarly, the unreal appearance of the three doctors who 'floated downstream on a raft' marks this poem as a fantasy that reveals the frustrating feelings of helplessness felt by the poet in the face of human suffering ('The Wound'). Finally, the poet is reminded of his own mortality by means of the dream fantasy concerning the reading of his own obituary ('The Saint'). Each of these poems uses the fantasy as the device by which the ideas of the poem gain expression. By the use of fantasy in these poems McFadden is showing the precarious nature of human existence in view of man's physical mortality.

The poetic devices that McFadden uses in all of his work tend to simplify the presentation of his message. The use of simple prose-like colloquial verse, of specific reference to cultural attitudes, of direct statement and the reportage technique, among others, are simplifying devices that McFadden uses not only to observe the real nature of the society in which he lives, but also to offer, by implication, valuable social criticism. On account of this simplicity, some critics have thought that McFadden writes trivial poetry and have criticized him for a lack of profundity.[12] This criticism is misdirected, however, because these devices, in view of their presentation of even the simplest aspects of the physical world, remain true to the poetic vision McFadden first declared in *The Poem Poem* and established in his subsequent works. To make the poem 'well-wrought' would be false not only to his poetics but also to the vision that he has of the world in which he lives.

¹ George Woodcock, "Swarming of Poets" in *Canadian Literature*, 50, Autumn 1971, pp. 3-16.

² David McFadden, *The Poem Poem* (Kitchener, Ontario: Weed/flower Press, May 1967).

³ Douglas Barbour, "Reviewed", in *The Canadian Forum*, 48 (May 1968), pp. 44-45.

⁴ David McFadden, *Letters from the Earth to the Earth* (Toronto: Coach House Press, 1969).

⁵ This criticism has been made by D.H. Sullivan in *West Coast Review*, October 1970, pp. 69-72. Analysis that is contrary to this view and supports the above assertion has been made by David Helwig in *Quarry* XIX: 2, Winter 1970, pp. 59-60, and by Joseph Sherman in *The Fiddlehead*, November/December 1969, pp. 64-66.

⁶ Vancouver: Talonbooks, 1975.

⁷ David McFadden, *The Great Canadian Sonnet* (Toronto: The Coach House Press, 1974). All quotations from this book are taken from this edition.

⁸ This analysis is supported by Frank Davey, *From There to Here* (Erin, Ontario: Press Porcepic, 1974), pp. 182-185. It is the only critical analysis that deals with either *The Great Canadian Sonnet* or the important difference of theme that exists between McFadden's novel and his poetry.

⁹ David McFadden, *Poems Worth Knowing* (Toronto: The Coach House Press, 1971). All quotations from this book are taken from this edition.

¹¹ David McFadden, *A Knight in Dried Plums* (Toronto: McClelland & Stewart, 1975). All quotations from this book are taken from this edition.

¹² Criticism of this nature has been made by Ralph Gustafson, "Circumventing Dragons", in *Canadian Literature*, 55, Winter 1972, pp. 105-106; and Lazar Sarna, "Aims Apart", in *Essays on Canadian Writing*, 3, Fall 1975, pp. 63-65.

Frank Davey: Finding your voice: to say what must be said: the recent poetry.

Douglas Barbour

Relatively recently, as the galaxies turn, a number of new books by Frank Davey, including a ten-year retrospective collection, ended up on my desk. Davey has been writing poetry, polemics and criticism since 1961, when *Tish* first informed the rest of Canada that poetry was alive and noisily well on the West Coast. Along with George Bowering and a number of other young poets who collected around *Tish* at various times in the sixties, Davey produced a large volume of work, and wrote widely and hotly to defend the poetics espoused by the *Tish* group, at least in the public's mind. He produced four books before 1966: *D-Day and After, City of the Gulls and Sea, Bridge Force,* and *The Scarred Hull.*[1] Then after a four year silence he burst back upon the scene with two books in 1970: *Weeds,*[2] and *Four Myths for Sam Perry.*[3] *l'an trentiesme: selected poems 1961-70*[4] followed in 1972. That same autumn, his powerful poem sequence *King of Swords*[5] appeared. *Arcana,*[6] a collection covering the years 1964 to 1970, and thematically linked to *King of Swords,* appeared early the following year. As I was about to sit down to write this article, his latest book, *The Clallam,*[7] arrived. There is also a small, privately printed poem, *Griffon.*[8]

I want to devote most of this article to the recent work,

starting with the 1970 books, and focusing on the poetry of *King of Swords*, *Arcana* and *The Clallam*. In order to demonstrate its value, and the immense strides forward it represents for Davey's personal poetics, however, I must devote some space to the early poetry. How helpful, then, that Davey chose what he now considers the best representative poetry of the early sixties for *l'an trentiesme.*

As has been,[9] or will be,[10] well documented, the *Tish* poets were primarily influenced by Black Mountain poetry and poetics. The personal visits by such Black Mountain figures as Charles Olson, Robert Duncan, Robert Creeley and others, their readings and discussions, both public and private, in the Vancouver area during the early sixties, put an indelible stamp on the poetry of a whole generation of West Coast poets.[11] Nor was this necessarily a bad thing, for the dedication, integrity and energy with which they pursued poetry brought a similar energetic intensity into being in the poetry emerging from Vancouver and environs at that time. However "good" we may consider that poetry now, it marked a necessary beginning all involved can look back to with a certain pride.

Still, as Davey's own criticism has always insisted, an evaluation must be attempted. For me, then, although their hearts were in the right place as far as poetics went, their early poems are interesting today for only two reasons: 1) to reveal the immense creative energy that was suddenly unleashed among such a comparatively large group of young writers-in-the-making; 2) to reveal how far the best of that group have come in the intervening years, growing each into his or her personal poetic voice.

The central theoretical statement for the *Tish* group would have to be Charles Olson's famous essay, "Projective Verse,"[12] which could be found in the seminal anthology of the early sixties, Donald Allen's *The New American Poetry, 1945-1960.*[13] I don't intend to go into great detail about Olson's poetics, as they are probably well enough known. His ideal of a truly organic, "open form" poetry became the ideal of the *Tish* group as well. Nevertheless, as is true of all apprenticeships, the group's early poetry appears much more written to formula than anything else. The result, in Davey's case at any rate,[14] are poems which seem, even at their best, to be not much more than five-finger exercises, as "Angoisse" demonstrates:

> That dark fuzzy-haired girl
> coming in a College Library door
> > > > (from the rain)
> is looking at her two cream galoshes
> (I hope)
> At least
> that is where her eyes
> > > > are pointed
> And I
> foot forward door riding shoulder against the glass
> am committed
> > > (does she know)
> to going out
>
> > > > > (*l'an*, 5)

The lines are broken correctly, the perceptions do, I suppose, follow, one upon another, but, and this is surely the most cutting thing one can say about a poem, Who cares?

My personal feelings towards nearly all of Davey's pre-1966 poetry is Who cares? Although they look fine upon the page, and reveal an obvious intelligence at work, these poems fail to grip either my emotions or my imagination. Nevertheless, even in this period, certain signs of growth can be charted. The fairly long (4 pages) poem, "Victoria," tries valiantly to make a powerful moral statement via an historical meditation upon the legend of Camosun (*l'an*, 26-29). I think the poem's power rests more upon its idea than its execution; somehow I know I should care more than Davey succeeds in making me care. At this point, I should make it absolutely clear that I believe style *creates* content, when we understand content to stand for *everything* the poem *says*. My complaint, therefore, is a stylistic one: Davey's language is neither rich nor complex

67

enough to realize the statement the poem can be seen to be groping towards.

Nevertheless, a poem like "Victoria," or the poems about ships wrecked off the coast of Vancouver Island which formed part of the sequence, *The Scarred Hull*, and now stand as separate poems in *l'an trentiesme*, reveal a desire on Davey's part to extend the range of his poetry, and to explore certain local Canadian roots for his art. Indeed, although *The Scarred Hull* also fails to move me enough, its attempt to mix the stories of the ships and the stories of handicapped schoolchildren is a sign that Davey's conception of the poem's innate possibilities was expanding. The two aspects of the sequence never do mesh into one poem, however, and the individual ship poems are too much like journalism to succeed even by themselves; Davey, the objective reporter, once again fails to involve us because he is seemingly not that involved himself. He would not return to the subject of old shipwrecks until 1972, with *Griffon*. Finally, in *The Clallam*, he would handle it in a marvelously complex fashion.

Davey's published silence from 1966 to 1970 is of interest only because the collections which followed that hiatus represent such a major step forward for his craft. *l'an trentiesme* contains some of the poems from *Four Myths for Sam Perry* and the whole *Weeds* sequence. The choice is a good one, if only because I feel he correctly left out all the weak poems from *Four Myths*.

Four Myths is a collection of poems, organized into four sections: "Amulets," poems about poem-making; "Sentences of Welcome," basically political statements; "A Light Poem," a powerful sequence based entirely on an exploration of the imagery of light; and "Sam," two poems meant to mythologize the Vancouver filmmaker, Sam Perry. Davey has reprinted "A Song to Mary" and "The Making" from "Amulets"; "Watts, 1965," which I don't particularly like any more than any of the other poems from "Sentences of Welcome"; and "A Light Poem." I wish that, instead of "Watts, 1965," he had reprinted "For Her, A Spring," because it is an interesting early attempt to connect the personal and the political: a love poem, especially in "ii," it creates both love and poem in metaphors, using repetition in an interesting manner.

The use of repetition for a specifically tonal effect is new in Davey's work at this time, and is especially effective in the two poems from "Amulets," poems which seek a personal ritualistic approach to the act of poem-making.

The poems in "Sentences of Welcome" fail mainly because they appear to be written *to* an already held political position. They therefore fail by Davey's own standards:

It is my view of myself and of many of my friends here at *Open Letter* that there is a place in the writing of poetry for *discipline* and *control*. And not at all a small one. But *discipline* and *control* are never in any way to be applied to the poem; rather they are to be applied to the poet himself. It is our view that the poem, like the short story, the novel, the dance, the piece of sculpture, has its own laws, its own directions, its own disciplines, and that these are to be strictly submitted to by the poet rather than ignored in favor of his own predilections. Again, the possibilities for the letter and the poem are open, infinite. And yet as soon as the poem begins its first phrases it has already begun to select from that infinitude, to close the possibilities. The poem's rimes of rhythm and tone become actual as the poem becomes actual; the true poet will ignore his secret cravings for the memorable poem, the ornate poem, the clever poem, or the reputation enhancing poem, and discipline himself to follow these rimes, and to provide only for their fulfillment. This is the only kind of discipline permissible in the writing of poems, the self-discipline of the man before the word.[15]

This is a very important statement, for, if Davey was not capable of living up to it when he wrote it, it was, and is, a noble ideal, and one he began to approach more and more in the following years.

Indeed, "A Light Poem," of all the poems in *Four Myths*, comes closest to achieving it, for Davey follows each "light" rime where it leads him, and succeeds, as he does not in "Sentences of Welcome," in convincingly exploring personal and political meanings of "light" without preconceptions. When the poem finally leads him, and us, to the humane blindness of a "Johnson, or / Lt. Calley, who created / in their own dark imaginations / a shadowless land / . . . / a floodlit / lucidity," (*l'an*, 80) we can believe the insight is gathered, not planted. In its attempt to connect the personal to the public or political, "A Light Poem" looks forward to *King of Swords* and *The Clallam*, though those are two very different poem-sequences.

"Sam" contains two poems that appear to be too planned; the careful use of sexual imagery, for example, is just too careful. Moreover, Sam Perry is presented in these poems as a figure of legendary dimensions, yet we have only the poet's rather shrill insistence to go on. I finally did not believe the assertion, although I did believe the sincerity with which it was made.

In the same year as *Four Myths*, Davey brought out *Weeds*, one of Coach House's exquisite examples of book-making. A 26 part serial poem, it represents an essentially new and mature exploration of word-rime combined with an extension, in practice as opposed to theory, of the idea of concept-rime. An organic poem-sequence, and perhaps that is the fairest short definition of a serial poem available, *Weeds* explores the major image/metaphor of the garden in all its complexity throughout the 26 sections. Simultaneously, a number of lesser images occur at various points, thus forging further important links in the sequence.

For *Weeds*, Davey adopts, most of the time, a long, very loose, poetic line. I can't agree with one reviewer who said these were prose-poems, but the general length and gentle rhythm of the lines does move towards prose while never quite falling into it. One of the ways Davey avoids prosaicness is through a new use of repetition within each section of the poem, as in these lines from "Motions," #5:

I cannot think in terms of windows, glass
beads, hurld, hurling at me in a perhaps dimension. It is not even a dim world today. It is just
the same, outline, outline, plane on plane, the
winter trees black, motionless, the sky no more
than window. Words too flow from my lips
inaudible. Escape. These escape. Ink lines dark
against a shallow page.

(l'an, 47)

Weeds concerns the aftermath of a break-up. The
persona, alone in his garden, looks back on the relationship, sees how it destroyed both lovers, and slowly,
through the central metaphors of weeds and poetry,
comes to some understanding of it. For the reader, the self-
conscious poetic awareness of the persona promotes
understanding of, as well as sympathy for, him. The weeds
of the title, for example, appear quite early, in #6:

And the garden, it grows weeds. They
spring from the very rendings of the soil that
mark where the old weeds grew. So hard not
to think of. 'A weed,' they say. Tear it up, tear
it up, the shock of weeds growing, of me following, weed to weed to catch them all, & what,
what can they mean for the garden.

(l'an, 48)

As they recur, in the various real and legendary gardens
the poem invokes, their connotations of vibrant, chaotic
life, the denial of chains upon creativity in nature or in
poets, for which they speak, becomes clear. And these
chains, the too-well tended garden, is what this marriage
had become.

There is much more I would like to say about *Weeds*,
much more I would like to quote, but it is not absolutely
necessary. In many ways it is a most accessible poem, for
the "story" it tells is only clarified, never obscured, by the
careful use of images and metaphors throughout. The
move to a new, dangerous, garden on the ocean's floor in

#25 is shockingly right, the near-concrete chant of #26 a marvelously appropriate conclusion to a sequence in which the very human ambiguities of the situation being explored are embodied, always, in concrete imagery of archetypal force.

As I have already mentioned, the poems of *Arcana* range all the way from 1964 to 1970. Most of them, I believe, are from the latter part of that period, for only one "manuscript" poem is dated 1964, one 1965, the rest from 1968 to 1970.

Arcana is in many ways a very personal book, verging on the confessional. Yet, because of the poetics implicit in Olson, Duncan, and other Black Mountain poets, it never approaches the kind of confessional poetry associated with Robert Lowell and his followers. Nevertheless, through the ingenious device of printing "manuscript" poems, earlier discarded as not worth revision, Davey manages to publicly articulate some very private matters concerning both his poetry and his life. Once they are mixed in with the more "finished" Tarot-influenced poems which make up a large portion of *Arcana*, moreover, these discarded "manuscripts" take on a new life, informing and being informed by the surrounding work. By some alchemy of context, they achieve a poetic worth Davey originally could not see in them.

The "story" of *Arcana* is a familiar one: a sterile marriage destroys itself, and a new, fruitful love replaces it. It is, in fact, an extension of the "story" of *Weeds*. Much of the mythic dimension of this collection comes from the Tarot and its powerful associations. *Arcana* does not structure its argument too tightly; the poems are carefully organized, nevertheless, to evoke the change of seasons, the change of marriages, yet each poem is a self-contained entity, and many of them are brilliantly evocative on their own terms.

"For Australopithecus," (*Arcana*, 54) for example, contains the kind of lavish connections across vast spans of time that recall Al Purdy's similar tricks. If it is more bookishly learned as befits a more bookish poet, it is nevertheless a compelling and moving poem. "Manuscript, 4 December, 1970" (*Arcana*, 55) is an early study, perhaps, of certain major themes of *King of Swords*. Titled "The Emperor," it uses meaningful word-games to sing a Tarot-inspired dirge:

The king leads armies who are emblems of
his leading. Emblems of bleeding, whose arms are
arms raised to raise his arms to kingdom. The
soldiers dream of vineyards in their marching
rising. Of the foe marching the king's emblems
raising. The king dreams of fucking the women
of the foe to love. The villages blaze with love.
The amazement in the dead children's eyes eyeing
the love he is loving.

Arcana concludes with poems celebrating the new wife's pregnancy and the birth of their son in March, 1970. The final poem in the book is "The Mirror." It is "a serial poem abandond 16 March, 1970" (*Arcana*, 63), and it contains some brilliant sections. Those on the act and art of poetry are important statements of Davey's present poetic, as well as good poems in their own right. Thus, in "Is There No Climate," he says:

To let one's words bespeak one's condition
at the moment of speaking. A poetry. I would be
that careful. That careful. Does no one
believe me? Why are the words frozen? Have I
in my willfullness, making poems of events
& poems of ideologies, frozen
my tongue, frozen
the waters around my child's skin?

(*Arcana*, 68)

Later, in "Habit," he images it even as he struggles for a meaningful escape:

Not to have it. Not to have the poem
when the habit won't let you have it.

73

Possesst by habit. A living that reproduces
the days of its living. Or poems that reproduce
the pages of past living. Not to live
but to be lived. Inhabited.

Let me not read poems. Let me not learn
poetics. Let me detest
images of my words in journals,
anthologies, in all those places
where habit is habit, let me not love
competence, heroism, idealism, I am not
competent, not heroic, not idealistic,
I cannot change a goddamn tap washer, or cry
upon a photod corpse —
I am only
a writer, struggling to hear his own
words, speaking.

                                                    (*Arcana*, 72)

"The Mirror" is important in Davey's development
because so many major obsessions of his poetry are wittily
engaged within its words. As the conclusion to *Arcana*, it
stands, as it should, making no apologies, seeking no easy
ways out of our common dilemma of being human, and
articulating with marvelous clarity the explorations such a
stance implies.

Even a close reading of the poems of *Arcana* might not
prepare one for the sustained power and range of *King of
Swords*. This is a complete serial poem, in 40 parts, and for
its tightness, its craft, it is about the only poem I have come
across recently that is worthy to be mentioned in the same
sentence with Phyllis Webb's *Naked Poems*. Though they
are very different poems, each a poetic expression of a
particular vision, they do share a concern with love, loss,
the individuals involved, and the questions such involve-
ments with others raise. Such a comparison cannot be
carried too far, of course, for Davey explores the political,
in the widest sense of that word, consequences of these
concepts, while Webb explores their more private philosophic and aesthetic dimensions. But then, the last thing

we need is a copy of *Naked Poems*: that work stands alone as a great original poem. Davey's does, too.

In *King of Swords*, Davey sustains a painful examination of the power politics of love and lust through a brilliant merging of narrowly personal concerns and historical and mythological archetypes. Where *Weeds* looked at love and its destruction solely in terms of the garden archetype, *King of Swords* surveys the same ground through Tarot images and the great narrative image of the whole Arthurian story. And with what sharpness he connects that beautiful story to the present day, not only to his disintegrating marriage but to all of us in this society, and in so doing reveals that it is precisely where we see the greatest beauty in it that it is most dangerous to us:

v.
The battle at Bedegraine — all
those young boys — Sir Griflet,
King Clariaunce, Sir Kay,
Gwimiart de Bloi —
cock-proud, cunt-blinded.

If only they had killd him,
their king — instead
driving their lances
into the bowels of horses,
sparring with broken beerbottles,
switch-blades — letting
their blood to embroider
royal flags, ladies' bosoms,
Modern Romances.

Though the poem is in no sense *actively* feminist, it certainly supports a feminist vision:

ix.
Onward we go,
riding into the sexual dark.
Lot, Pellinore, Gareth,

Gawain — our pricks
remembering Arthur's seed. To Uther,
his father, there was no other grail
than Igraine's womb. Disguised
as her husband, he enters. How
we all dream of that moment.
The rapist's glamour.

For afterward she loves him.
The husband, they find,
has been conveniently killd
in the night. Their child
king of Britain.

Davey clearly shows how invalid the great images of
Romance are to our survival, both psychic and physical,
today; or, at least, he shows how carefully, and with what
subtle understanding, they must be invoked. To do this, he
intercuts images of destructive love, "Imagining yourself
pregnant / four months running, & in the fourth / scaring
your own blood from its flow / until our wedding day" (xiv),
with images, newly seen but always there, from the
Arthurian legend:

  xvii.
Mordred, born:
& Arthur, told by Merlin
only that his slayer
is a babe that May,
continues to die, gathering all
the knight's & lords' children
of that month
— 4 weeks old & less —
setting them adrift in a ship
to wail, & die.

The "flower of chivalry" —
fuck the women, murder the babes.

Davey's learning serves him superbly in this poem, and yet, like Robert Duncan's, it never gets in the way, it is absolutely natural: how else could he say this? The "poem's rimes,"[16] the riming that emerges naturally from following the poem unselfishly, is what *King of Swords* offers. Merlin and his pride, too great not to allow Nineve to trap him, the grail, Lancelot's story, all emerge from the poem in their proper place, connect with the present, with the whole historical vision, add their weight to the poem's total presence.

The grail, for example, is next mentioned in xxi: "So long to realize what / the grail was. Particularly, / not you." xxii is a superb mixture of medical quotation on the uterus and scholarly association with some of the most dangerous ladies of the myth. For the rest of the poem, the grail weaves in and out of the images, until the poem realizes, in the final sections, just precisely what it is.

Meanwhile, the violence implicit in "chivalry" is further explored. Sir Balan, "Only his blood-tipt sword / pointing onward" (xxvi), is immediately connected to a car crash where the poet, having rushed out of his home to the scene, can see only "an ear-ring chaind / to the rear-view mirror / but not his face. For his blood / lay on the inside of the shatterd windows / emulsified with moonlight, engine oil." (xxvii) Such viscerally apprehended connections form the core of the poem's argument concerning our divided, violent, sexist cultural heritage.

So that the statement of xxxvi comes as no surprise, is terribly right, is terrifying in its implications and yet holds out the faint hope that if we can recognize its awful truth we might begin to change, to find our way out of this historical, cultural wasteland:

& the death of Arthur continues.
His knights, your knights
joust tonight in Belfast,
lead armies, now, August 21, 1971,
in Bengla Desh, Sudan,
have begotten, ten years in Saigon
100,000 orphans of chivalry.

For just previously, in xxxv, the poem clearly articulates its basic insight:

Prick, cunt — my god, not
weaponry. *Please, if you forget*
the King of Swords, he will die.
Then the dish, the cup
will bear water, & even the staff
stand, sprout leaves, branches. (my italics)

Knowing this, and living in proper relationship, or trying to, with his new love, the poet can see the land return to fertility, a natural way of life, the weapons now truly ploughshares:

xxxix.
My new love's belly too
becomes, with care,
a cornucopia

as I watcht it thrust
not steel, but our blood, out
into the breathing air.

The sequence ends in just three lines that transverse history, myth and personal life; and none is imaged forth concretely for all to perceive:

xl.
Corbenik.
'Cor benoit,' blessed
horn.

Even such a cursory reading as I have given it reveals the range and depth of *King of Swords*. It stands as the central achievement of Davey's career thus far, a triumphant bodying forth of his poetics in action, and a powerful emotional experience of the kind we associate with truly good art. Yet, *King of Swords* does not stand apart from his other recent work, but is closely connected to the poems of

Arcana and *Weeds*. In all three books, Davey's learning, his ability to mass and use a vast and scholarly range of allusions, finds expression in a personal and often deeply moving poetry, a unified vision with no pedantic overtones. It is their idiomatic strength that makes these poems so immediately accessible to the reader, forging emotional connections that will not be denied.

It is this powerful bonding of the historical/mythical with the personal that is missing in the early poetry, even where the poet attempted it. The ten years separating *D-Day and After* from *King of Swords* are years of apprenticeship to poetic craft as Davey slowly came to perceive it. They are also years of deep learning, in both the personal and scholarly senses. When the two merge, with a profound sense of the poetic act as exploration, as the seeking out, selflessly, of the poem's own rimes, unimposed, the results are explosive: a *King of Swords*.

Like *Naked Poems, King of Swords* is unrepeatable. Both in its particular form, and in its particular statement,[17] it marks an end, and therefore, necessarily, a new beginning. In the *The Clallam*, Davey returns to his interest in the shipwrecks off Vancouver Island. *The Clallam* is so much stronger and better a poem than those collected in *l'an trentiesme* because Davey can now involve us personally, through his own feelings, in the documented disaster.

The Clallam was an American boat which sank in Juan de Fuca, causing the deaths of some four dozen Canadian passengers, bound back to Victoria after a Christmas holiday in Washington. Davey quickly pulls us in:

> There are documents
> but no objective witnesses
> of *The Clallam's* sinking. The survivors
> were not objective. I
> am not objective. Only
> the objects we survive in.
> All the stinking white corpses.

Davey makes us share the anger he feels now, so many years after the sinking in early January 1904. This is a sea-story, a poem in a great Canadian tradition of documentary poems on the sea, but it is a mean one, about a mean man, Capt. George Roberts, who had taken no insurance on the ship he had sunk his savings in, and therefore tried to make it through without accepting offered rescue so as to avoid extra costs from his own pocket. For Roberts, "even goddamn Ned Pratt would have put away / the Scots metaphor —" this no Prattian epic of men working heroically together for some larger cause.[18] Rather, it is a savage document of human selfishness, of cowardice and base immorality concerning one's passengers.

Mixing documentary fact, evocative images of sea, snow, and storm-tossed ship, and personal moral outrage, Davey creates a powerful collage, in which human depravity shows clearly, but not without some few acts of courage and goodness to remind us that this is a document of individual men, not mankind. The poem as act of homage is also presented, as well as the human uselessness of such an act for the dead passengers: "The sound of words as they fall / fall away from our mouths. / Fog, bubbles."

Once again, the rimes ring true: the facts, the terror of the drowning people, the acts of courage and kindness, of meanspirited denial of human truth, the poet's own violent expression of anger that this should be, weave in and out organically throughout the book. All moving to the final, obscene, revelation:

Our portrait of Capt. Roberts
six months after: a free
man. Avoiding Canadian land
& waters. License
temporarily suspended.
Having done nothing, we conclude
contrary to U.S.
custom or law.

The final page, when it arrives, has the inevitability of an oracle observed:

The ship American
the builder American
the captain American
the survivors American.

This is a controlled anger, and a further insight into how countries get along, to the despair of individuals perhaps, but who can be bothered about that? Perhaps it is the poet's duty to be so bothered, at any rate *The Clallam* seems to say so.

It is impossible to say what direction Davey's poetry will next take. He now has both the talent and craft necessary to his enterprise, and that is all that really matters. On the basis of his recent work, I can only say I look forward to seeing whatever he does, for I feel sure it will be interesting, satisfying poetry, a poetry shaped by the poet's deep sense of how poetry must naturally emerge from the roots of place, time, and personal knowledge, commitment and feeling. Frank Davey has found his voice, and it is a powerful and original one, one I look to hear from again.

[1] In order: (Oliver, B.C.: Rattlesnake Press, 1962); (Victoria: Morris Print Company, 1964); (Toronto: Contact Press, 1966); (Calgary: *Imago* 6, 1966).

² (Toronto: Coach House Press, 1970).

³ (Vancouver: Talonbooks, 1970).

⁴ (Vancouver: Vancouver Community Press, 1972).

⁵ (Vancouver: Talonbooks, 1972).

⁶ (Toronto: Coach House Press, 1973). The vagaries of little press publication should warn us not to take these dates too seriously. *Arcana* had been with Coach House a considerable time before it was finally published.

⁷ (Vancouver: Talonbooks, 1973).

⁸ (Toronto: Massasauga Editions, 1972).

⁹ Beverley Mitchell, S.S.A., "The Geneaology of *Tish*," *Open Letter*, 2/3 (Fall, 1972), pp. 32-51.

¹⁰ Warren Tallman has been promising a collection of essays on the West Coast poetry scene from McGraw-Hill Ryerson for a few years now.

¹¹ In fact, Davey wrote his Ph.D. dissertation at the University of California on the theoretical bases of the poetry of Olson, Duncan and Creeley.

¹² In *Human Universe and other Essays*, ed. Donald Allen (New York: Grove Press, 1967), pp. 51-61.

¹³ (New York: Grove Press, 1960).

¹⁴ Quite frankly, a glance at the early issues of *Tish* reveals that all the young poets involved with that "poetry newsletter" are equally apprentices to their craft. Though no better than the others, George Bowering was the first of the group to become known, and he is still the most talked-about member of it. One reason I am writing this article is to argue that Davey's recent poetry is equally deserving of comment and appreciation as Bowering's.

¹⁵ "More Heat on Daedalus," *Open Letter*, 1/8 (November, 1968), p. 27. See, also, "Rime, A Scholarly Piece," in *The Making of Modern Poetry in Canada*, eds. Louis Dudek and Michael Gnarowski (Toronto: Ryerson, 1967), pp. 295-300. This is a major statement of the theories of rime alluded to in the passage quoted.

¹⁶ "More Heat," p. 27.

¹⁷ I want to make absolutely clear that although I often talk of a poem's "statement" or "argument," I do so only because it seems unavoidable. As I have said, "form" or "style" *creates* "content" in a most meaningful manner. One shouldn't talk of them separately, but it seems we can't avoid it. *King of Swords'* total form is, let me repeat, all that it says, the full experience it creates for us.

¹⁸ Davey is one of the few critics who has attacked Pratt's poetry, and his is a very careful and well-mounted attack on the vision of man Pratt's poetry upholds. See his "E.J. Pratt: Apostle of Corporate Man," *Canadian Literature*, 43 (Winter, 1970), pp. 54-66.

The Poetry of George Bowering

Ken Norris

"Consciousness is how it is
composed."

(George Bowering, *Autobiology*)

To consider George Bowering's poetry is to ultimately
wind up talking about language and the processes of
writing. If one were to approach Bowering's poetry from a
thematic viewpoint one would still find that the nature of
language and the relationship between the poet and the
language would be the touchstone of discourse; Bowering's prevailing "theme" is language itself and how it
works. Whether the poems under consideration are the
early lyrics, the explorations of *George, Vancouver,
Autobiology* and *Curious*, or the Steinish verbal play of *A
Short Sad Book*, it is the writing process which exists as
the primary field of attention. A survey of Bowering's
writing becomes a study of the principles of language at
work: the subtleties of cadence and rime, the use of the
lyric or serial poem form, the associative way in which
language sometimes unfolds, as well as Bowering's use of
the poetic breath line and rambling prose line.

An original member of the Vancouver *Tish* newsletter
group, Bowering willingly acknowledges the poets of the
American Black Mountain school as having been a primary

influence upon his writing. All students at UBC in the early sixties, the *Tish* group coalesced around Warren and Ellen Tallman who had contacts with the San Francisco poetry scene; it was via this connection that poets such as Robert Duncan, Robert Creeley and Jack Spicer wended their way north to provide instruction for the novices of Vancouver. Serious about the craft of poetry and eager to learn all they could, the *Tish* group absorbed the lessons of their American teachers. Duncan's theories of language, Creeley's precise minimalism, the essence of the Beats as embodied by Ginsberg, Jack Spicer's notion of "dictation" and his writings in the form of the serial poem, and Charles Olson's "Projective Verse" essay were all seminal to the poetic development of these young Vancouver poets. *Tish*, a newsletter of poetry and especially of poetics, documented what had been learned in the poems and essays of *Tish* editors Frank Davey, Jamie Reid, David Dawson, Fred Wah and George Bowering. The early issues of *Tish* illustrate in their contents the absorption and trying out of new theories of poetry with which the young Canadian poets had been presented. The obvious point to be made about the *Tish* group is that they distilled the majority of their influences from American rather than Canadian sources.

An off-shoot of *Tish* was Tishbooks which published the first pamphlet-type volumes of poetry by Frank Davey (*D-Day And After*, 1962) and George Bowering (*Sticks & Stones*, 1963). Bowering's *Sticks & Stones*, with a preface by Robert Creeley, indicates, as do his early poems in *Tish*, his immediate overriding concern with the process and practice of composition. The first poem in the collection, "Wattles", suggests metaphorically how composition begins:

sticks & stones

you begin to build

　　　　from moments
　　　　of strictest energy
　　　　upwards

The sticks and stones are words, the building blocks of language. Implied in the connection between words and sticks and stones is their sparse and solid object nature, the starkness and weight that they embody. From the very beginning Bowering's poetry is one of noun and verb (with a Creeleyesque emphasis also placed on prepositions and conjunctions) rather than of adjectives. The presence of the poem is conveyed by the thing itself embodied by the noun, recalling a statement that Spicer made in one of his letters to Lorca in which he said that he wanted the lemons in his poems to be real lemons; the action and kinetic energy of Bowering's poems rely upon the motion of verb rather than the enhancements and pyrotechnics of adjectives to propel them. In this manner his poetry avoids the overworked slushiness of traditional and academic verse.

Much of the poetry collected in *Sticks & Stones* is obviously the work of a young poet. The awkwardness that one finds at times, however, is not in the workings of the language but rather in Bowering's approach to his subject. The book contains an interesting mix of poems that fail to generate any sustained interest and several poems that are extremely strong pieces. The poem "Cadence" considers how the music of the poem is made while, at the same time, providing that very music:

so that it is the walking of the voice

the

opening of doors and the walking
on floors
and the closing of doors

the swinging of arms

and the talking of the voice

As lyric poet Bowering also shows a considerable ability with the love poem; "I Ask Her", "Wrapped in Black", "Eyes

85

That Open", and particularly "The Sunday Poem" all
capture a lyrical tenderness:

I love your
                    mystical overnight opening
of the flower
                    autumn purple
reflected lights in your
noon day sun day eyes

                              So that
                              I catch
my breath

                              (lungs full of midnight air
                              :the overnight opening)

                              I swear
                              there are
pieces of pollen
in the air you breathe into my lungs

                                        ("The Sunday Poem")

The hesitations of the first stanza reflect the sense of
wonderment that the words themselves are trying to
capture; the short breath lines of the second and third
stanzas embody the shortness of breath that the poem
itself is speaking of, so that there is a perfect synthesis
between what the poem is saying and the breath line and
cadence with which it is said. This seemingly simple poem
reveals itself as a poem of more than simple composition.
The poems in *Sticks & Stones* show an intense awareness
of craft. When a poem fails it is because the words fail to
deliver enough meaning; the prosody of the poems is
sound.

Practically all of the poems in *Sticks & Stones* (a book of
limited circulation) reappear in two subsequent volumes —
Points On The Grid (Contact Press, 1964) and *The Silver
Wire* (Quarry Press, 1966) — among newer pieces. Like
Sticks & Stones, *Points On The Grid* is a mixture of poems
that shows a technical competence but fails to click and

poems of real accomplishment. "Radio Jazz" is one poem that fulfills its potential, recreating the music the poet hears over the air waves in the deft lines of the poem:

Sucked into the horn of the jazz
on lonely midnight Salt Lake City radio
over to me alone in a big house
hundreds of miles in the mountains
fantastic piano then
key to me right hand left hand on silent radio sound
on a million radio America waves in the dark

The modulations of the long lines recreate the sense of music transmitted by way of radio waves and the words create a sense of musical color that is "jazzy".

The poems in this collection again present the process of language as the focal point of Bowering's poetry. One is continually aware of the breath line and the need for the poem to be sounded, read aloud, rather than be kept flat upon the page. The poem on the page exists purely as a score, to suggest how the speaking voice should articulate it. In several poems, as in "For A", Bowering begins to adopt a Creeleyesque breath line, a foreshadowing of the minimal line he would use throughout most of the lyrics in *The Man In Yellow Boots* (El Corno Emplumado, 1965), his finest collection of early lyrics. In "For A" the language is simple, brief, and direct:

what joy
to teach you joy
of love

a little
at a time

what fun too
our one
little find
at a time

how dear
the simpleness
of it

how thank you
how thank me

for each
syllable
we say of it

In reading the poems contained in *The Silver Wire* one is
impressed by how adept Bowering is at writing the short
amatory lyric. Towards the beginning of the book there are
a dozen or so love poems for his wife Angela, all of which
share a precision and simplicity of imagery and manage to
evoke a genuine sense of tenderness and wonder. They
are real love poems, real celebrations:

Here is Angela's
hair on the side of
my face; love as

clean and soft as
it is immediate
to me.

("rime of our time")

Look at me long enough
and I will be a flower
or wet blackberries dangling
from a dripping bush

Let me share you
with this flower, look
at anything long enough
and it is water

("inside the tulip")

Although one is primarily struck by the love poems in Bowering's early work, *Points On The Grid* and *The Silver Wire* contain several of Bowering's much anthologized poems: "Locus Solus", "Grandfather", and "Circus Maximus". An interesting thing to note about *The Silver Wire* is that it contains the poems "Ed Dorn", "Phyllis Webb", and "Red Lane", short studies or sketches of poets which foreshadow Bowering's later, more ambitious collection of poets' portraits: *Curious*.

It is *The Man In Yellow Boots* that contains the finest work of Bowering's early lyric period. A special issue of the bilingual (English and Spanish) *El Corno Emplumado*, edited in Mexico City by Margaret Randall, *The Man In Yellow Boots* is a collection that engages itself with the realities of love, politics, and language. Of the political poems many fail to get off the ground; much of Bowering's overtly political writing has always been rather heavy-handed and clumsy. In love poems like "To Cleave" one is impressed by the clarity and verbal sharpness of the poem:

When I enter you
you enter me.

That is to cleave,

to cling,
cut,

penetrate
& love.

Three longer poems stand out as the poems of real achievement in the collection. "For WCW" successfully utilizes Williams' poetic forms to celebrate his poetic accomplishments and pay honor to the poet himself. Bowering uses the identifiably Williamsish variable foot triple line throughout much of the first and fourth sections of the poem; in the second section he adopts Williams' minimalist couplets while in the third section writing in an idiosyncratic wandering and variable line structure that occasionally appeared in Williams' poetry. Bowering adopts Williams' speech, "American/language shouting/ across the Potomac", to pay tribute to Williams. Bowering views Williams' poetry as

Language lifted
            out of the ordinary
                        into the illumination
of poetry.
                        Objects: sticks & stones
                                    coming together
you place before
            our eyes
                        exposed bare to the weather
rained on and
            crackt dry in the sun

A stick a stone
            a river cutting thru clay
a white barn in a field
                        a cat coiled
                                    on a box

("For WCW")

The tangible concreteness of Williams' poetry is a quality that Bowering himself has developed in these early poems, and is a quality he continues to employ; Williams' dictum "No ideas but in things" is a basic poetic principle to which Bowering has always adhered.

The poem "The Descent" echoes a Williams poem of the same title. A reminiscence of Bowering's father, it reverberates with a sense expressed in the poem by Williams: "Memory is a kind/of accomplishment,/a sort of renewal/ even/an initiation, since the spaces it opens are new places".[1] Bowering's poem is a long one, the process being one of Bowering seeing his predecessor in himself: "When I think of him/it is me—" he states at the beginning of the poem. The reminiscence that occurs in the poem becomes "a sort of renewal", a process of self-discovery.

In the poem "Esta Muy Caliente" Bowering adopts the

form of the descriptive anecdote, a form that is usually very loose and casual; Bowering keeps a tight rein upon it. The poem is organized into four line stanzas and is written, as always, with precision and an exactness of language. The poem describes an event: Bowering and company as tourists have to stop their car near San Juan del Rio in Mexico to let a funeral go by. The procession, with its music and cherry bombs, is accurately described, re-creating an atmosphere that mixes mourning with an almost strange rite of celebration. The last two stanzas provide a pivot upon which the poem turns:

An hour later the road was clear
and as I got in the car
a man on a donkey came by
a San Juan lonely in the mountains man.

Good afternoon, I said.
Good afternoon, he said, it is very hot.
Yes it is, I said, especially for us.
It is very hot for us too, he said.

Contained in this seemingly ordinary verbal exchange exists a certain intangible illumination that is a precise characteristic of poetry.

The lyrics contained in *The Gangs Of Kosmos* are the poems of a poet who is no longer a novice; these lyrics, and those contained in the suites *Rocky Mountain Foot* and *Sitting In Mexico*, represent the beginning of Bowering's mature work. This second lyrical period is marked by Bowering's absolute surefootedness. The occasional awkwardness of the early books is gone. The subjectivity of the lyric form ceases to be marred by personal misjudgements of taste that arose in Bowering's early efforts. The subjective voice of the individual is now overseen by the objectivity of an accomplished poet. There is a greater lyrical concentration in the poems, a greater effort being made to keep the melody of the poem in tune and non-digressive, and to keep the kinetics of emotion fixed and rooted in creating a single, unified

91

impression. "The Boat", from *The Gangs Of Kosmos*, is a
perfect lyric poem:

I say to you,
marriage is a boat.

When the seas are
high enough to
turn us over

we must hold
not one another
but our own positions.

Yet when the water
is calm under sea moon

we can even stand up
& dance
holding tight, each to each.

The achievement apparent in *The Gangs Of Kosmos* and
Rocky Mountain Foot was acknowledged by Bowering
being awarded the Governor-General's Award for Poetry
for these two books. Although working in the lyric mode,
these two books point out Bowering's increasing interest
in the longer poem. Among its short lyrics *The Gangs Of
Kosmos* contains two longer pieces, "Windingo" and
"Hamatsa", which are based upon Indian legend. "Windingo" explores the spiritual form of the North, a lurking
shadowy monster with a heart of ice, while "Hamatsa"
probes an Indian legend which tells of the origin of an elite
group of human flesh eaters; in an affecting way Bowering
relates this legend back onto the reality of the poet living in
modern day Vancouver. The latter poem represents a
strange interweaving of the primitive and mythic with the
present in an attempt to establish or discover the spirit of
place of the west coast. In this kind of poetic activity we see
in Bowering's writing a movement out and away from
personal concerns toward a greater concern with the

specifics of the sacredness of Canadian geography.

Rocky Mountain Foot is a suite of lyrics that takes the province of Alberta as its place. The poems consider the geography of the province, sitting at the foot of the Rocky Mountains, note the climactic changes of season embodied by winters of snow and summers of dust, and delve into the history and social conditions of Alberta. Bowering intersperses his poems with quotations from various indigenous texts: newspapers, historical treatments, studies of the badlands, and the statements of prominent Albertan politicians of the past and present days. *Rocky Mountain Foot* shares with some of the poems contained in *The Gangs Of Kosmos* a searching into of outward reality, of that which lies beyond the personal. The process of these poems is perceptive rather than proprioceptive; one sees the poet as being in the place and observing it rather than the place being ingested and the sense being made within the poet. In poems treating the mixed Albertan atmosphere of oil and sand, and in describing the social conditions of the province Bowering is very much the commentator. These poems reflect less of a personal involvement than the early lyrics and later serial poems. *Rocky Mountain Foot* is the fruition of Bowering's desire to express a social and political self; having achieved this, his later work returns to a certain introversion in which the poet confronts the possibilities of language *as* language rather than as a conveyor of message and meaning. *Rocky Mountain Foot* is, in many ways, Bowering's most polemical work.

Sitting In Mexico, which was the 12th issue of *Imago*, Bowering's magazine devoted to the long poem or poem series, like *Rocky Mountain Foot* is a suite of individual poems that work together to evoke the spirit of a place. At times the poems in *Sitting In Mexico* approach the tight weave of the serial poem; there is sometimes a strong inter-relationship between the individual lyrics. *Sitting In Mexico* is much less ambitious that *Rocky Mountain Foot*; however, in its simplicity, it occasionally succeeds more in evoking the atmosphere of Mexico than *Rocky Mountain Foot* does in evoking Alberta, despite the fact that the individual pieces in the latter book are, on the whole, much stronger. Again, like *Rocky Mountain Foot, Sitting In Mexico* is a collection that sees the world with an outward turned eye. The poems are often the embodiments of perceptions about the specific characteristics of Mexican life.

What is indicated by Bowering's attempts to work in a more extended form was his growing dissatisfaction with the simple form of the lyric. By the late sixties he had begun to seek a larger structure: that of the book. *Rocky Mountain Foot* and *Sitting In Mexico* point towards Bowering's concern with the book length poem or serial poem. His last two collections of lyrics, *In The Flesh* and *The Concrete Island*, have been compilations of remaining uncollected earlier work rather than a continued working within the lyric mode. Both of these books have been prefaced with statements which have declared that Bowering's primary poetic concern is now with the serial poem. These last lyrics have been presented as the final products of a stage that Bowering has since outgrown. Although the poems maintain a proficiency of style and technique they often reflect a lack of interest. Clearly, Bowering's consciousness, beginning in the middle to late sixties, began to be intrigued by and fixed upon the phenomenology of the serial poem.

Bowering's best and most interesting work has been written in the form of the serial poem, a form popularized among poets of the Pacific coast by American poet Jack Spicer. The guiding principle of the serial poem, as Spicer saw it, was the process of "dictation", a process in which the poet surrenders up his control over the poem. Spicer believed that what happened in dictation was that "instead of the poet being a beautiful machine which manufactured the current for itself, did everything for itself — almost a perpetual motion machine, of emotion, until the poet's heart broke, or was burned on the beach like Shelley's — instead there was something from the outside coming in".[2] During his Vancouver lectures, Spicer defined the basic structure and workings of the serial poem:

A serial poem, in the first place, has the book as its unit as an individual poem has the poem as its unit, the actual poem that you write at the actual time, the single poem. And there is a dictation of form as well as a dictation of the individual form of the individual poem. And you have to go into a serial poem not knowing what the hell you're doing. That's the first thing. You have to be tricked into it. It has to be some path that you've never seen on a map before. I think all of my books as far as they're successful have just followed the bloody path to see where it goes, and sometimes it doesn't go anywhere. What I'm saying is you have to have a unit, one unit the poem, which is taken by dictation, and another unit the book, which is a more structured thing. But it should be structured by dictation and not by the poet. And when the poet gets some idea — oh, this is going to amount to this or going to amount to that, and he starts steering the poem himself — then he's lost in the woods. And the brambles are all about. Or else he pulls out a boy scout compass and goes back to the nearest bar.[3]

Bowering's first book-length poem, *Baseball*, is, significantly, dedicated to Jack Spicer. An early Coach House book, *Baseball* was printed in the format of a baseball pennant. The poem is subtitled "a poem in the magic number 9", is written in nine sections, concerns itself with the nine innings of play, casts the 9 Muses in the role of today's line-up, and pays tribute to Bowering's favorite ballplayer of all time, Ted Williams, who wore the number 9 on his uniform. How much Bowering adheres to the principles of dictation in this poem is questionable. Several sections of the poem are reminiscences of sandlot and minor league ball that Bowering had witnessed; one gets the feeling that the controlling intelligence behind this poem is still that of the poet. Yet, for the lover of baseball and poetry, that fact is insignificant. The poem is a successful invocation of the spirit of baseball and links baseball with poetry through the connection of the magic number 9 and by way of the gracefulness and ability required in both disciplines. Poetry and baseball both rely upon similar skills. Addressing Spicer in the text of the poem, Bowering says:

> This story is for you, Jack, who had eyes to see
> a small signal
> from the box
> > more than 90 feet
> > away.

It's quite obvious here that the specific reference, though adopting the metaphor of baseball, is to poetry. At the heart of baseball is a certain aesthetic which the poet Bowering has picked up on:

> > What are you doing, they ask,
> > young esthete poet
> > going to baseball games,
> > where's your hip pocket
> > Rimbaud?

> I see the perfect double play, second baseman in the
> > air legs tuckt
> over feet of spikes in the dust, arms whipping baseball
> on straight line to first baseman, plock of ball,
> side's retired, the pitcher walks head down quiet from
> > the mound.

When the perfect play or perfect pitch occurs in baseball it contains the same magic that the poet is trying to capture in the poem. The game exists as more than a pastime; the final lines of the poem bring this fact home:

> > I want to say
> that it is not a
> > diversion of the intelligence,
> a man breathes differently
> > after rounding the bag,
> history, is there such a thing,

                              does not
choose, it waits & watches,
                              the game
isn't over till the last man's
                              out.

   Though Bowering may wonder in the poem *Baseball*
whether there is such a thing as history, in *George,
Vancouver* there is no question that history is something
that truly exists. The poem takes as its historical basis the
exploration of Burrard Inlet and Georgia Strait in British
Columbia by Captain George Vancouver. The historical
focal point is Vancouver's charting of his explorations;
another layer is added to the poem in that the poem itself
deals with Bowering's "discovery" and inquiry into the
reality of these historical facts. The subsequent "charting"
that takes place is both the process that George Vancouver
follows as an explorer and that his contemporary counter-
part, George Bowering, charts within the context of the
poem. Their mutual labor, as Bowering puts it forward at
the beginning of the poem, is

To chart this land
hanging over ten thousand inlets
& a distant mind of as many narrows

At the heart of the poem and the historical incident exists
"the relationship between fancy & the real". Vancouver
was sent out to discover a water passage across British
North America on behalf of the fanciful English king, who
was looking for a route to send his men across the new
continent to protect his interests in the Pacific region. In
contrast to the king's fanciful desire we are presented with
the concrete tangibilities of Vancouver's exploration of the
inlets and his charting of them, and the botanical research
of Archibald Menzies, the ship's botanist, who spent his
time making drawings of plants, collecting seeds, and
keeping an accurate journal in which he recorded
diseases, places, and vessels that were anchored off the
northwest coast. Ultimately, Vancouver recognizes that

the king's northwest passage will never be found and that

> We'll all go home
> the long way, empty-handed
> but for my charts
> & his weed-book.

The relevance of this information to Bowering is that it informs one of the actual presences and contours of the British Columbia coast, defining a sense of place rather than being the fulfillment of fanciful and abstract speculation. The poem itself jumps through time, from the reality of 1792 when Vancouver's explorations took place, up to the present day in which the contemporary George inhabits the territory that Vancouver had charted. Through his tracing of Vancouver's discoveries Bowering himself begins to develop a stronger sense of the place in which he is in. When, towards the end of the poem, he writes

> Let us say
> this is as far as I, George,
> have travelled.

he is speaking for himself as well as through the voice of Captain George Vancouver. The physical geography and the process of mind have both been "toucht, sighted/mapt to some extent,/the islands/noted."

The writing process that Bowering adopts in *Genève* is an interesting exercise in phenomenology. Using the 22 cards of the major arcana and the 16 court cards of the Geneva Tarot pack, Bowering shuffles the cards and turns them over one by one, registering his immediate reaction to the image with which he finds himself presented. The chance order of their appearance provides the overriding structure for this interesting serial poem. The poet's blindness to the poem's direction and his willful relenting of control again ties in with Spicer's conception of the way in which the serial poem works:

Robin Blaser once said in talking about a serial poem that it's as if you go into a room, a dark room, the light is turned on for a minute, then it's turned off again, and then you go into a different room where a light is turned on and turned off. And I suspect one of the reasons that makes people write serial poems is the business if you can get focused on the individual part enough you have a better chance of dictation, you have a better chance of being an empty vessel, being filled up with whatever's outside.[4]

The image of a light being turned on and then off is quite apt in relation to the process of *Genève*. The card is turned over, the image is presented in a moment of illumination, to which the poet registers his reactions, and then the card is retired and chance must provide the next image which creates the sequencing. Bowering quite consistently and deliberately steers away from engaging himself in the poems with the level of interpreting arcane meanings and the history of the cards. He relies purely upon the imagery of the card to trigger his internal reaction which produces the poem. Often the poems describe the component parts of the visual image and then register the reaction. A preponderance of male swordsmen at the beginning of the process produces a string of meditations upon struggle; drawing cup cards Bowering finds the cups to be ultimately empty. The final card drawn is Death: a significant last card to end the series. What intrigues the reader more often than not in *Genève* is the process of poetic engagement rather than the poems themselves. Many of the poems, looked at individually, are quite weak. The strength of the serial poem and the interest that it generates is that the book, as a whole, is often greater than the sum of its parts. This is very much the case with *Genève*.

Autobiology is the first of two books in which Bowering adopts a repetitious and rather incantatory prose line with which he writes his book length poem. As the title of this book indicates, the approach that Bowering takes in the telling of his life is through reference to the physical self, this physiological mode providing a very real insight into the consciousness which, in essence, defines the writer and his writing; as Bowering notes several times in the course of *Autobiology*: "Consciousness is how it is composed". By exploring his physiology Bowering comes the closest one can to exploring the self that inhabits the body; he records the influence or impression that accidents, broken bones, scars and other physical injuries that happened to him have affected upon his sensibility. The eighth chapter of *Autobiology*, "The Breaks", illustrates both the subject concern of the poem and also the method of composition:

Before I broke my nose the first time it turned up & I wisht it did not turn up & I got my wish. Before I broke my nose the second time it had a hump & I wisht it had no hump & I got my wish. Before I broke my nose the third time I was not reconciled to having a funny nose but I made no wish because I'd seen what that leads to twice but it broke again anyway. Before I broke my nose the fourth time I wisht I would break something else for a change & I got my wish. Before I broke the middle finger of my right hand I was working hard in the orchard & I wisht something would happen to me & I could quit working for a while & I got half of my wish. Before I broke my foot I wisht something would happen beyond my control to get my girl & I into bed together & I got a portion of my wish. Before I broke my hand I wisht I could impress my intended with the sincerity of my emotion & we got my wish.

Those are the breaks. We make our own breaks. We learn to take advantage of the breaks. We step on the breaks. We apply the breaks. The breaks even themselves up. We dont ask for more than our share of the breaks. Those are the breaks of the game.

Bowering's method in *Autobiology* is proprioceptive, a process which Warren Tallman, in interpreting Olson's difficult terminology, sees as a modus operandi in which "*Self*, having subjected itself to its surroundings, becomes the *Subject* of a new writing which it is easiest to define as a *Life Sentence*. Self is the subject, writing is verb and the object is life, to be as fully alive as one can manage by way of sight, hearing, thinking, feeling, speaking — that is, writing".[5] This is certainly the case in *Autobiology*. Bowering develops a sense of the self as having been subjected to its surroundings, to the point of having been impinged upon by a series of multiple injuries. The subject of *Autobiology* is very much the physical self and the process of action is the process of writing itself. Often the poet recollects and thinks with the poem as he is writing it; the writing process serves to illumine and express the state of liveliness of the individual. At the heart of this process of life and writing is the attempt on the part of the poet to crack the code of his own consciousness, which, in turn, becomes the method for composition. In discussing *Autobiology*, Bowering has noted the connections that link the physical occurrences with consciousness and then to poetry:

> *Autobiology* deals with everything that happened to
> . . . not everything, but a lot of things that happened to
> me physically and physiologically that formed my mind
> the way it happens to be now, and the mind is what
> makes poetry happen.[6]

It is the mind's ability to call up recollections of past physical reactions and injuries that provide one impetus for the generation of the writing. The repetitive quality of Bowering's prose lines also serves to provoke the mind to recall past incidents and make connections which become the structural principle upon which the poem is based. The different chapters reverberate with certain key incidents to which the poet's mind gravitates and which become the touchstones of the poem, having obviously played a major part in the development of Bowering's consciousness and physical sense of self.

Written in a prose line similar to that of *Autobiology*, *Curious* is a collection of 48 "portraits" of poets, filtered through Bowering's consciousness. The disclaimer that appears at the beginning of the book — "The characters in this book are all creations of the author's imagination. Any resemblances to actual people, living or dead, are purely coincidental" — is a hip joke, but also indicates that the poems do not work by way of a realistic point by point correspondence. These portraits of poets are proprioceptively made; they are expressed to the extent that Bowering has inwardly sensed these poets' existences. Some poets, like "David McFadden" and "James Reaney", are extremely imaginative and fanciful, in a way being take-offs on the aesthetic sensibilities and personalities of the poets. Others ("Charles Olson", "Charles Reznikoff", and "Margaret Randall" are examples) work within the mode of the anecdote, to which is added the poet's personal responses and interpretations. Perhaps the most powerful piece in the book, "Charles Olson", is a telling account of an encounter with the leading theoretician of the Black Mountain school:

> He was coming down the stairs so large he was
> coming down the stairs so tall I thought he
> is so large it is the stairs coming down on
> our heads or I thought in a way he is
> still coming up the stairs & we are at
> the bottom & here he is. I introduced myself
> & I was looking at his belt buckle which
> was crooked. The stairs were behind him
> but they could not be seen so we will
> never know where he came from or how
> he got there, so big. He is so big we are
> in awe of him but he was always giving
> large pieces of himself & we never call him
> by his name made short he was so tall. A
> friend today said he never understood anything
> he wrote or said & my wife said there is
> an honest man. I said I understand lots &
> lots I don't understand. I lookt at his belt
> where he would have to buckle to be our
> size & some of us would have him do that
> but not many. Older than Byblos earlier than

Palestine & possesst of an alphabet before
the Greeks he came down on our heads
like buckling stairs. He said hello & said
this must be Angela but he didn't remember Angela has yellow hair at least in
the poem. The words enter at the eyes &
meet their neighbors there & eventually know
everyone there, a polis behind the eyes. Hello
he said, neighbor, on this other coast. Years
later it was true but it was always true.
Old clothes years later other old clothes he
dresst in all the language we could ever
have had. Hello he said at the bottom
of the stairs where we were, it was
startling though we had heard of the size
that was all in books where the words were.

In that Bowering does not seek to make normal prose
transitions, i.e. explanations of where the writing is now
going, changing time or incidents, he enables the writing
to move closer to the process of thought. In the piece the
primary time frame is an occasion upon which Olson
descended a flight of stairs and said hello. Around and
through this Bowering weaves a series of other elements.
His incantatory invocation of Olson's largeness makes one
aware of the physical size of the man but also of the stature
of Olson as a poet, a poet towering over other poets as he
towers over other men. Interjected into this description is a
conversation at a later point in time between Bowering and
a friend about their ability to understand Olson's writing.
Like associative thought the piece then returns to the
primary incident with Olson saying hello and "this must be
Angela". The poem does not pause to say that Angela is
Bowering's wife or to explain just exactly which poem it is
in which she has yellow hair. Instead there is the continuity
of flowing thought and association. Bowering uses this
method in an attempt to get to the immediacy of
experience and impression, to simulate the actual workings of consciousness as it happens. As he notes in the
poem "Frank Davey": "Literature is telling the story, as it

happens". In *Curious* Bowering strives to bring consciousness and composition to the point where they are both happening at once. Although the poems in *Curious* are written in a prose line they are poetry in how they occur, how they connect. The logic of discursive prose is supplanted by a spontaneous poetic reaction which does not attempt to explain the process of thought but rather to embody it.

In *At War With The U.S.* Bowering returns to the use of a verse line. A serial poem consisting of 34 sections, *At War With The U.S.* is a poem that has, at its heart, the spirit of political and cultural protest. Throughout the poem we are made aware of the U.S.'s Southeast Asia war effort (the poem having been composed between January and August of 1973), the violence and aggression of which Bowering condemns. There is also implicit in the poem the sense of U.S. domination over Canada, both in economic and cultural terms. Going into a cafe to get real french fries only to have them come out of a frozen bag, Bowering knows where to place the blame:

> You nighted states I know you
> are responsible for this, & I know
> if I sprawl dead a minor martyrdom
>
> the bowling alley coffee shop will be
> mixing scum into the ground beef patties
> in McCook Nebraska while they
> take my corpse away &
> puzzle my baby daughter's frowned-over eyes

Bowering, in the course of his writing and in conversation, has often noted that, when he was growing up, he always felt himself to be an American rather than a Canadian. The influence of the American Black Mountain poetic upon him is also to be noted. In attempting to get out from under the cultural domination of the U.S. it has been necessary for Bowering to declare his own personal war upon the States in an attempt to free himself from its influence:

At war with the U.S.

I surrender

I embrace you

Now
get off my back

Stand
in the light
where I can see you

This poem marks a momentary return to a poetry of
political concern which was much in evidence in Bowering's early work. Bowering's latest prose work, *A Short Sad
Book*, bears a relation to *At War With The U.S.*, in that it
seeks to provide a cultural narrative for Canada.

Allophanes is a long extended serial poem which truly
reads as if it has been "ghost-written" or "dictated". From
the first line of the poem, "The snowball appears in Hell/
every morning at seven", which Bowering heard intoned
by the voice of Jack Spicer, the poem is a visitation of
voices. The poem does not refer to but rather speaks of and
through Dante, Yeats, Joyce, greek myth, alchemy, Jewish
mysticism, the Imago Mundi, and the holy city of Byzan-
tium among others. In this way the poem is an illumination
of European philosophy and mysticism. The "appearances" of these spirits and voices glimmer and shift hue as
do the colors of mineral formations, a process to which the
world "allophanes" is scientifically applied. In many
respects *Allophanes* is Bowering's most Platonic work, in
that it would seem to find its resolution not in the things
themselves but in some divine sense of order. The poet, in
this poem, is clearly the agent or medium through which
the voices are allowed to speak. As Bowering self-
reflectively notes:

You've tried it & tried it
                    & it cant be done, you

cannot close your ear—

(I)

The voices must be listened to and recorded, though they speak through a veil of obscurity, for by way of obscurity one may come to the illumination: "the obscure lies necessary to the luminous,/to make seeking take place of the random" (III). For Bowering, the obvious way through to any understanding is by way of the language; for this reason he advises the reader to

Have a seat on my language
& here we go,

lecherously, thru the flowing world
of Hera's clitoris.

(IV)

The pun here is upon Heraclitus whose notion it was that you can't step into the same river twice, that the world is continually in a process of flux.

The poem is, in many ways, a maze of thought and philosophy. Neither the reader nor the poet is ever quite sure of what exactly is taking place. From where Bowering stands his reaction is that "If you don't understand the story you had better tell it" (XI). He is not in control of the poem, consciously guiding it, constantly directing the flow of the language. Instead, the process of dictation is fully at work:

I felt something strike me.
I fell on something.
With a shape something like my own.

The language
is not spoken
it speaks.

(XXIII)

Because it is the language that speaks there is little explanation, often very tentative connections between sections and even between juxtaposed stanzas. Parenthetically stepping into the poem for a moment, Bowering can only advise the reader to

> . . . shore up the fragments
> for yourself, dont expect
> fullness here, I'm only
> one pair of ears.)

(XXIV)

Allophanes does not present the reader with a "fullness", a sense of an ordered and resolved poem; instead the reader finds himself watching the subtle changes of color and appearances that take place within the cave of thought and perception that the poem frames.

Whether working within the mode of the lyric or the serial poem Bowering has tried to actively engage himself in his writing with the on-going processes of living and consciousness. His poetry is, at heart, processual, being kinetic rather than static; the poems capture a certain life energy within the bounds of a form that suits them well, rather than being works of artifice.

[1] William Carlos Williams, *Selected Poems* (New York: New Directions, 1962), p. 132.

[2] Jack Spicer, "Excerpts From The Vancouver Lectures," *The Poetics of The New American Poetry*, ed. Donald M. Allen and Warren Tallman (New York: Grove Press, Inc., 1973), p. 228.

[3] Spicer, p. 233.

[4] Ibid.

[5] Warren Tallman, "Wonder Merchants: Modernist Poetry in Vancouver during the 1960's," *Godawful Streets of Man* (Toronto: *Open Letter*, 3rd Series, No. 6), p. 194.

[6] George Bowering in interview, "Curiouser & Curiouser," *CrossCountry*, no. 5, p. 19.

Perceiving It As It Stands:
Daphne Marlatt's Poetry

Robert Lecker

It is difficult to read Daphne Marlatt's poetry[1] without
seeing the river. Behind each of the books she has
published to date, there is a current which flows toward a
heightened perception of an immanent world. The current
joins each of her works, swelling into the torrent of
impressions, sensations, and images which characterize
Steveston. Linked to this inherent proclivity for movement
is a need for poetic progress: each book can be seen as
representing some form of search for an appropriate
language of relation, for a form of discourse which will find
a centre and render in clarity the instantaneous apprehension of things and thoughts caught in flux:

> shapes flutter
> glide into each other
> but the hand
> wanting to know
> picks a thing
> out from the center

Marlatt is involved in a quest for words which will give
access to the truth of sight, reflecting not only the moment,
but the dynamic nature of experience and cognition. She
arrives at a torrent, but not overnight. In fact, much of the

power (and sometimes the weakness) of her earliest work lies in the tension between tentative, frightened spontaneity, and an ambitious, robust control. So that in her first book, *Frames*, we find her hesitant about the plunge into this river of experience, content at first to watch this movement called Life from the sidelines, as if it were a show:

I'm/ on the sidewalk viewing the procession.

Gradually, she compromises, slowly immersing herself in the flow, thereby allowing *Frames* to become more than simply a poeticized version of Andersen's "The Snow Queen". Marlatt reinterprets a number of the tale's motifs, and uses these to define and call into question her own situation as a poet. The result is an allegorical prose-poem dealing with a search for a form of aesthetic freedom in the face of limitations imposed by style and personal experience. The first lines acquaint us with the themes of imprisonment, escape, and search, while the book at large elaborates upon these themes by examining them in the context of restrictive private and aesthetic frames.

The protagonists are Kay and Gerda, two next-door playmates living in attic rooms. Through the frames of windows decorated with boxes of roses they watch each other watch each other. Sometimes Gerda visits Kay, and listens to his grandmother's stories. Clearly, Kay and Gerda lead a life dominated by images of enclosure which limit and structure their experience of the world. Grandmother's stories constitute the most potent image of confinement, for her words belong to a paralyzed, strictly ordered past divorced from process and liberty:

She hypnotizes me with the past fulfilled, always filled, as if that should be enough

Until Kay and Gerda and Marlatt herself are "lockt/ in the grandmother's stopt voice", and left with no alternative but to survive through fleeing into a story of flow which

endeavours to obliterate the incarcerating influence of
dead words and frozen time:

> (at your grandmother's
> time is a glacier, bodies of ancestors keep turning up in
> the shadows of afternoon . . . But here, if anywhere, is
> a way out there

Marlatt has every right to join Kay and Gerda in flight, for
their predicament, and the development of their story,
serve as a metaphor for the problems of growth encountered by a poet struggling to break away from the frames
imposed by established word patterns and the falsities
implied by a worldview which categorizes experience,
storytelling it in standardized form, as if the motion of
living was always the same, always sane. Marlatt is not
opposed to absolutes, but to the belief that absolutes can
exist in isolation. Throughout her works, she insists that
experience is a matter of relation. Hence stasis is validated
by movement, stability assumes meaning in the midst of
chaos, the individual realizes himself through others.

Frames represents Marlatt's initial attempt to formulate a
poetry which would establish a correlation between perception and articulation. The task she immediately sets
for herself is that of seeing herself seeing the world. She
expresses a desire to unite the arts of seeing and telling in a
bond so intimate that the eye will be interchangeable with
the mouth:

> as far as the eye can tell . . .

Or, she sees herself as a digester of word-phrases-as-food,
reorganizing, assimilating, and occasionally regurgitating
the words, purging herself through the creation of new
pictures which originate in the depths of her system:

> thrown up
> on each other in a
> room word pictures be
> come cru
>   /shall . . .

But she recognizes the difficulty of satisfying her own objectives, and in *Frames* we witness the struggle involved in achieving a balance between language and the reality it tries to describe. Because that balance never quite materializes here, language still manages to subdue the expression of reality, resulting in a strange mixture of fantasy, dream, and fact.

Significantly, both children are driven and controlled by the implications of language, and Kay is immediately presented as the victim of words which affect him in the same way as the fragments from the demon's distorted mirror do in the Andersen tale:

from this we know
two mirror chips divide
love
    his vision of love
eyes
his heart

Kay suffers from the effects of a selective vision which ignores and destroys totality. Consequently, he cannot realize the complete poetic vision which, Marlatt implies, is composed of a blending of sight and emotion, heart and eye. The phrases which Grandmother casts upon Kay hypnotize him into believing that reality is the story itself, and so he is blinded to process and the world, stripped of his emotions, becoming a slave to the "Snow Queen" heroine whose tale has overcome him.

Marlatt sympathizes with Kay's plight, for it signifies many of the constrictions that she herself is trying to avoid. More important is the fact that she identifies with Gerda, whose activities assume the form of an aesthetic quest for experience inspired by a thirst for discovery. In the process of her quest for Kay, Gerda reads and interprets a phenomenological universe of signs which direct her towards the object of her search. Marlatt seems to admire Gerda's ability to leap into a flow of experience, and she emphasizes the power of the child's eyes, which are like nets capturing the multitude of images which comprise experience:

Can she see her seeing net

> sight, light
> start out of her eye!

There is an obvious envy of Gerda's camera-like eye, photographic in its ability to objectively capture the progression of moments constituting her search:

> tells her tale
>   caught
> in camera obscura of her
> history, an image
> of the search

Clearly, one of the problems in *Frames* centers on Marlatt's dependence upon a character called Gerda:

> Gerda, you'd better believe it! I'm clinging to you

Marlatt's reliance upon Gerda suggests a reluctance to assume her own voice, and a fear at the thought of challenging the river alone. At the same time, she wants desperately to discover the child's sense of wonder and immediacy, to move into Gerda's world of relentless and varied experience. So like a child she cries:

> Let me come too!

And she does go, but their voyage ends in failure. Although Gerda manages to locate Kay, the poetic release ostensibly to be derived from the movement towards cognition never materializes. The story ends much as it began, with Kay and Gerda once again depicted as prisoners:

> Back to back to the room. Where
> windowboxes with roses border their image of the world.

Any suggestion of the fairy tale is destroyed, and reality

returns more heavily than ever, accompanied by a sense of defeat. On one level, the defeat is an aesthetic one, engendered by Marlatt's knowledge of the fact that she has relied upon the medium of Kay and Gerda to transmit her own experience of the world. Like them, she has tried to escape a frame imposed by words, but ultimately she admits the impotence of her own attempt. This aspect of the poetry is best revealed through an examination of the titles describing the seven sections into which *Frames* is divided. She is found, static, in (I) "white as of the white room", moving cautiously through (II) "shadows doors are" into colour and sunlight, where she experiments with poetry as painting in (III) "primary colours", gradually employing (IV) "light affects", and realizing (V) "visual purple". In (VI) "eye lights", the eye is defined in a play upon the painter's word 'highlight'. But in the last section, "Out a rose window", Marlatt renunciates all claims to what she herself saw as progress, admitting that her art, which depended largely upon a voice at second remove, never managed to progress beyond a semi-real word encounter with experience. So the image of the window and "containment (not content-)" is reinstated as Marlatt confesses to a lingering predilection for rose-coloured vision.

The story of Kay and Gerda serves as more than a metaphor for an aesthetic impasse. It also describes the very real personal crisis of a woman who has recently abandoned a difficult relationship which threatened to enclose her. In this sense the children can be seen as representing two lovers who have parted. While Kay demonstrates the cruelty of a man whose heart has turned to stone, Gerda is the epitome of a woman enslaved to the memory of a man whose visage continues to haunt her. The distinct note of pain involved in the thought of a snapshot-captured past is relieved only by the glimpses of freedom and weightlessness which are features of a developing individuality:

> But the whole weight of me shifted,
> changed value in fact. Without gravity I was absent too.

> Blown anywhere, clung to any personplace (for
> reprieval), had to begin to be a . . . will

It is this weight of the past which makes the act of seeing in the present so difficult to realize:

> knotted in remembrance, not . . . / seeing

The poetry of *Frames* may have frustrated its creator in her search for words and a style which would accurately reflect the sensation of being a consciousness in the world. But this does not detract from the fact that even in her first volume, Marlatt provides the reader with an example of creative brilliance and stylistic innovation.

One year later, in 1969, she returned to the public with *Leaf leaf/s*, determined to purify both language and image, and to resolve any discord between perception, voice, and experience. In her second book, Marlatt dispenses with any reliance upon fantasy or assumed voice, and somewhat resolves the conflict between stasis and fluidity by depicting consciousness as a series of instants comprising a flow, rather than as fragments and fluid which cannot mix. Here, she speaks in images as sharp and precise as photographs. Language no longer reflects upon experience, but *is* experience — the work is concise, immediate, distilled, demonstrating a variety of instantaneous responses to surrounding phenomena:

> that the
> summit of mountains
> should be
>
> hot at that much
> closer to
>
> ah clouds the
> sun

Each poem in the collection can be seen as an image which expresses an abrupt combination of the thing perceived and its effect upon the perceiver. These imagistic poems exist as entities, but they act as a leaf amongst leaves (leaf/s), or as part of a larger totality (tree of life?). The result is a set of perceptions which mirror a portion of Marlatt's awareness.

Leaf leaf/s appears almost as an exercise originating in reaction to *Frames*, and certainly, the reaction is complete. Whereas in *Frames* the syntax was often extended and complex, *Leaf leaf/s* presents a streamlined and extremely pure arrangement of language. Frequently, words stand alone as poems within poems, or as precious moments related to the whole through imagistic suggestion. The poem bearing the significant title "Photograph" is a good example:

> you sd a stalk I look
> like a weed wind blows
> thru
>
> singly
> smokes &
> fumes
> green's
> unripe a colour but
> elemental, grass
> easily hugs
> ground, that's you

Although Marlatt's second book resolves many of the difficulties connected with *Frames*, the feeling remains that there is an overreaction here, that by immersing herself so completely in the experience of a phenomeno-logical universe she ignores several of the questions of relation that remained unanswered in *Frames*. Marlatt is at her best when she qualifies an experience of the moment by relating it to time. A reading of *Rings* (1971) and *Steveston* demonstrates the intensity she can achieve by utilizing public and private history. Both of these later books are strengthened by their depiction of a poetic encounter with diverse forms of process and instantaneity.

In comparison, *Leaf leaf/s* suffers, for it is solely concerned with a singular experience of the moment abstracted from duration. Nevertheless, its strong images form a powerful part of the foundation upon which Marlatt constructs the success of her later works.

Rings immediately recalls *Frames* through its introductory metaphors of enslavement, but here, the notion of restraint is highlighted by contrasting images of hope, release, and birth. In one respect, the birth of her child reintroduces the heroine to a whole range of apprehensions which had been stifled in the silence of a difficult marriage. The re-entry of perception is accompanied by a shift in language that becomes more dynamic as the newborn child grows. Although the problems of wedlock are never resolved, there is a progressive emphasis on movement and increased clarity of vision, suggesting the development of a healthy state of control derived from the mastery of language in terms of relation. Now, Marlatt manages to organize and coherently employ many of the qualities which she sees as essential to the poetic act: process intermingled with definition through stability, self-definition realized with regard to seeing matched by an identical approach to the mode of being.

The first words of *Rings* give voice to the heroine's conscious state:

Like a stone

The initial image of weight and stasis gives way to a blending that establishes a correlation between the woman's stifled condition and the suffocating effects of a silent landscape and a brooding husband:

. . . smothered by the snowy silence, yours. Me?

This pervasive silence is quickly offset by a "jingling of rings", the symbol of an imprisoning marriage. Finally, a myriad of sensory impressions combines, working together to define the consciousness of a woman pregnant not only with child, but with the tensions of a strained marriage.

116

Characteristically, the fear of isolation-separation is linked
to a problem of words:

> My nerve ends stretch, anticipating hidden dark.
> I read too much in your words, I read silences where
> there is nothing to say, to be said, to be read. Afraid of
> your fear of the sea that surrounds us, Cuts off roads . . .

But this vision of being severed from the world ("disin-
herited from your claim to the earth") is relieved by the
waves of sun breaking through the window, and the
ensuing realization that sight has the ability to penetrate
barriers and join every object in a multilevelled vision of
movement and birth. As the sun "pierces glass (cold)
irradiating skin, water, wood", every sense converges in
the creation of a picture of hope, and the unborn child
"kicks, suddenly unaccountable unseen".

Rings "ii" continues to describe the woman's immersion
in a multisensory universe, but an interesting shift occurs,
for the barriers between inner and outer begin to disinte-
grate, making it difficult to distinguish between the seer
and what is seen. Marlatt's attempt to communicate the
belief that we are what we see finds its best expression in
this section:

> Back,
> back into the room we circle, It rings us. No, grows out of
> our heads like the fern in carboniferous light, smoke

The notion of perceptual and emotional intermingling
develops in the woman's mind until every fact of experience, from the past into the present, intersects in the
illustration of the functioning of a complex state of mind.
Marlatt's technical aims are also concerned with a blending, and so are governed by the belief in "image to outer"
— the conviction that there is a never ending equivalence
between landscapes of the world and mind.

Contained within the third section of *Rings* is the kernel
of Marlatt's aesthetic. First, the familiar river image is
evoked, signifying an ever-present state of flux and rela-

tivity, followed by a compact statement of the poet's concept of her art:

> Like a dream.
> There is no story only the telling with no end in view or, born headfirst, you start at the beginning & work backwards

The emphasis is upon discourse as a spontaneous act unhampered by structures of plot or duration. Yet at the same time, creativity and movement are made possible only through a process of self-discovery which involves an investigation of causality. As the woman meditates upon the child floating within her, a parallel is established between birth and creativity. The poet survives in the stream of experience only by continually relocating the origins of flow:

> 'delivered'
> is a coming into THIS stream. You start at the beginning & it keeps on beginning

Although fragmented language and images continue to illustrate the presence of a mulitphasic consciousness, the fourth section of *Rings* is primarily devoted to an examination of another relation: that between process, purgation, and birth. The metaphor is clear: creation can only be the product of a total release of consciousness. Spontaneity as a diarrhoea of words. The woman's desperate need for intestinal release is emphatically linked to the release provided by birth:

> if only
> it would all come out. But what if I had a baby in the toilet!

The greatest potential for poetry, however, exists in the actual movement involved in the process of birth, for only then is restraint destroyed to the extent that language cannot help but explode in expressing a tornado of sensation. No wonder the 'birth' section of *Rings* is the most intense writing Marlatt has done yet. Absolute abandonment to flow.

The rush of language is succeeded by a placid language reflecting a calmer emotional state. Through the birth of her child, the woman herself is reborn into a world of innocence. In her desire to fulfill the infant's needs, the woman finds herself imagining (imaging) and finally becoming his conscious state:

> this newborn (reborn) sensing, child I am with him, with sight, all my senses clear, for the first time, since I can remember, childlike spinning, dizzy

The section continues to evaluate the surrounding phenomena in a language as simple as childhood:

> this world. Something precious, something out of the course of time marked off by clocks

Reassembling the infant's astonishment. But not for long:

> cars whirr by outside, gravel spews. (A certain motor. Gears down, stops. News from outside coming home

Her husband's re-entry is matched by a return to more complex language and thought. Yet in the last section of *Rings* there is a sense of lingering tranquility, not because the marriage is better, but because the new child will add softness to experience. The book ends in an unsteady voyage away from the past and beyond familiar borders, suggesting the possibility of a marital recreation:

> How do you feel about leaving? for good. That question. (If it is good.   If we can make it so.)

The book's energy originates in the overall coherence that is established between a variety of conscious states, and in Marlatt's ability to realize a potent equation between sight, language, and thought.

Rings ends on a note of departure, to be followed by a

poetry of return and recognition. *Vancouver Poems* (1972) is a collection of highly polished sketches of city life, made vital by Marlatt's knowledge of Vancouver, and by the research she has done to enlarge upon that knowledge. A glimpse at the credits on the final page serves as proof of Marlatt's increasing concern with an "expanded vision" that sees the present with the aid of historical and socio-logical information. She is trying to discover an underlying myth which binds the poet into a ritualistic identification with the environment and its history. Consequently, we find poems inspired by the reading of such diverse sources as the *Vancouver Historical Journal, Art of the Kwakiutl Indians*, Weil-Brecht-Blitzstein, and *Vancouver from Mill-town to Metropolis*. The ritual is discovered as life itself, and the poet incarnates the ritual by becoming the word/world mouth which feeds on vision, growing on the nourishment of phenomena:

> We live by (at the mouth of
the world, & the ritual. Draws strength. Is not Secret
a woman gives (in taking, Q'ominoqas) rich within the
lockt-up street. Whose heart beats here, taking it
all in . . .

In these poems, Marlatt repeats her contention that the self can be understood only in relation to external phen-omena, and insists that "Matter inserts relation". Much of the book is devoted to the painstaking examination of the objects surrounding the poet. In fact, the success of Marlatt's effort is indicated by the difficulty which is inevitably encountered in any attempt to describe or classify the inexhaustible flood of images she incorpor-ates. This phenomenological inundation forces the reader to see Vancouver as a tangible reality. It also provides a lesson in the way we can visually restructure (re/see) our own surroundings.

In many ways, *Vancouver Poems* serves as the testing ground for Marlatt's latest book. Every facet of her skill as a poet is demonstrated in *Steveston*. Here (as the epigraph from James Agee indicates), she continues her avowed intention of "seeking to perceive it as it stands", creating word pictures which capture a set of momentary apprehensions. At the same time, she manages to blend those incredibly tight images with a flowing style that speaks for a Heraclitean experience of flux, discovering the voice which allows her to unite the acts of seeing and telling.

It seems only natural that in this volume, her poems are bound with (and to) Robert Minden's photographs, for her poems, as we have seen, always seek the precision, objectivity, and instantaneous image implied by the photograph, and her books are progressively characterized by an application of photographic principles. In *Frames*, she expressed her recognition of the imagistic power of the photograph, but tended toward the more traditional association between poetry and painting, perhaps because the snapshot then represented a verisimiltude that spoke with frightening ease about reality. *Leaf leaf/s* represented an attempt to create a group of imagistic poems possessing a photographic appeal to exactitude. Then in *Rings* we witnessed Marlatt's endeavour to improve the coherence between several 'exposures' of consciousness, and in *Vancouver Poems* she experimented with photographic impressions modulated by the introduction of personal recollection and historical data. *Steveston* is composed of a photographic poetry of immanence that improves upon the experiments of earlier works. But the book is much more than a refined expression of previous vision, for here, the maturation of Marlatt's voice is matched by a growth of self assurance that allows her to see herself in relation to a host of external questions. Throughout *Steveston*, Marlatt is continually examining the nature of her own poetic discourse, reminding herself of the need to remain attentive to the facts of physical reality:

> multiplicity simply there: the physical matter of the place (what matters) meaning, don't get theoretical now . . .

Steveston is the antithesis of that reluctant trickling which began in *Frames*. Now Marlatt has unquestionably

121

connected the story with a torrent of visual experience. For her, the book represents a visual reinitiation into life, and its structure describes an expanding rush towards a heightened understanding. At first, Marlatt confronts Steveston in the role of detached alien, capable only of seeing the town in terms of its exterior characteristics, or in relation to the publicized facts of its history. She knows that Steveston is the headquarters of B.C. Packers, but only in the course of her visit to the town does she realize the extent to which the canning industry has relentlessly exploited its resources, both human and environmental. In her desire to know Steveston's present, Marlatt begins by imagining the past of a town stricken by fire in 1918:

Imagine: a town

Imagine a town running
                        (smoothly?
a town running before a fire . . .

Movement begins with this step into Steveston's past. As her perception becomes more acute (and involved), she works her way through history into the present, arriving at a characteristic immediacy of sight. From an investigation of the general, she moves to a consideration of the particular, concerning herself first with industrial buildings and groups, and then with individuals, their jobs, their outlook, their home life:

                        To live in a place. Immanent. In
place. Yet to feel at sea. To come from elsewhere & then to
discover/love, has a house & name. Has land. Is landed . . .

As usual, Marlatt's perceptions transform her as she transforms through sight. In the end, the identification she realizes is so complete that she once again sees herself as performing the function of a mouth, giving voice to the sight of Steveston. Having assumed this primary role, she then associates directly with the mouth of the Fraser itself, indicating her willingness to spontaneously explicate and metaphorically become the very symbol of Steveston's lifeblood. She is "at the mouth, where the river runs, in, to the/ immanence of things".

This image of the poet-as-mouth-as-river is but another illustration of the repeated connection Marlatt makes between perception, digestion, and purgation. By allowing the phenomena which *are* Steveston to pass through her, Marlatt is able to 'digest' the town, regurgitating it as a purged verbalvisual image. Similar images of purgation appeared in *Frames* and *Rings*.

The resulting pictures of Steveston may be pure, but they are not pretty. Dominated by a disinfected, punctuated industrial routine, a multitude of immigrant workers find themselves enslaved and exploited by a packing plant that "packs their lives, chopping off the hours". Indeed, these people face the same fate as the fish which roll smoothly towards a mechanical death on the non-stop conveyor belts of productivity:

> . . . the blade with teeth marked:
> for marriage, for birth, for death

The mechanical precision associated with the factory also tyrannizes a community suffocated by an overdose of control:

> . . . & it all settles down into an order of orders . . .

Until consciousness itself becomes "silent, impassive", waiting in futility for an impossible release from an existence where "nothing moves", where even dream is shown to be an enslaved "pounding within the pound of machinery under mountains of empty packer/ pens".

The effects on an industry which thrives on the exploitation of human resources can be seen in an environment that is ravaged by pollution and destroyed through abuse. In this "decomposed ground choked by refuse, profit, & the concrete of private property", the inhabitants of Steveston live "as if the earth were dead/ & we within it ash, eating ash, drinking the lead fire of our own consumption".

But it is the Fraser River itself, "swollen with its filth",

123

"sewage", and "endless waste" that reflects in its stagnant waters the most exact image of a town gone sour. Ironically, the inhabitants must depend for their living on the very river whose pollution and decay symbolizes a human degeneration flowing sluggishly to death. Their "lives/ are inextricably tied with the tide that inundates their day", and so "there's a subhuman, sub/marine aura to things", with life seen as static, drowned. Every phenomenon in Steveston points to an overwhelming submergence and stasis exemplifying the predominance of impotence. This infertility is manifested in the undeniable absence of any form of material or human growth. There is only one growth:

> This corporate growth that monopolizes the sun. moon & tide, fish-run . . .

Like fish, again, these cannery workers are involved in a futile cyclicality which ends only in the grave. But Marlatt discovers an heroic element in the lives of these people who demonstrate a Sisyphean urge to survive:

> Somehow they survive, this people, these fish, survive the refuse bottom, filthy water, their choked lives, in a singular dance of survival, each from each . . .

Actually, *Steveston* can be seen as a historical, sociological, and geographical study of a region extending far beyond the bounds of Marlatt's consciousness. She moves outward, progressing beyond the Fraser to a vision of the sea. In order to facilitate this outflowing, she first seizes upon the minor phenomena which form the basis of a larger vision, ultimately defining herself in the light of others. Because she takes the time to trade stories with an aging fisherman, he "connects" . . . "when the young woman from *out there* walks in". After speaking with a Japanese sailor who insists that she's a hippie, Marlatt sees herself anew:

I'm clearly a woman on their float. Too weak to lift the

124

pole, old enough to have tastes

From "out there", she comes to us too, saying something
radically different, allowing us to see ourselves anew.
Definition, light (recognition) sight ... Marlatt adds detail to
detail (re)producing an onrush of purified visual discourse
that balances the moment in flow. She remains with the
river, writing poetry of immanence at its best.

[1] Daphne Marlatt, *Frames* (Toronto: Ryerson, 1968); *Leaf leaf/s*
(Los Angeles: Black Sparrow, 1969); *Rings* (Vancouver: Georgia
Straight Writing Supplement, Vancouver Series No. 3, 1971);
Vancouver Poems (Toronto: Coach House, 1972); *Steveston* (Van-
couver: Talonbooks, 1974).

Writing Writing: bpNichol at 30

Jack David

bpNichol is a writing phenomenon. At the age of thirty, when most writers are getting their first books into print, Nichol has published over ten full-size books and scores of pamphlets, been editor of Ganglia Press and grOnk, made three records, edited one anthology, been admired internationally for ten years, and won the Governor-General's Award for poetry in 1970. This is not to mention his many reviews and critical articles, some of which approach classic status as initial attempts to map out evaluatory criteria in concrete poetry. All in all, an outstanding beginning.

Only a full-length book could adequately deal with all of his writing. In this paper, therefore, I have selected representative samples from all Nichol's genres of writing and focused my discussion, as Nichol focuses his writing, on the question of writing itself — Nichol's attitude towards writing (apparent or implicit) being one of the keys to an understanding of his work.

Nichol's goal is to escape from the barriers of what Edward Sapir terms "a straight ideational language" in order to "return to the root elements of both the written and aural language." Sapir, Nichol's main source for this theory, also asserts that "ideation reigns supreme in language."[1] In order to counteract this domination, Nichol thinks that "something new must be done with words." One such possibility is to "leave the beauty out" of words, and another is to "begin again by breaking words up to let the staleness out of them."[2] Nichol explores both these areas in an attempt to break down the barriers which prevent poetry from achieving its full scope.

Traditional poetry is only one means by which to reach out and touch the other. The other is emerging as the necessary prerequisite for dialogues with the self that clarify the soul's heart and deepen the ability to love. I place myself there, with them, whoever they are, where-ever they are, who seek to reach themselves and the other through the poem by as many exits and entrances as are possible.[3]

Nichol's concrete poetry can be divided into two broad areas. First, there are typewritten or typographical poems which make use of the page's space and the letter's shape to create visual effects. Second, there are his sound poems, fully realized only on record or in concert reading, but sometimes reproduced in printed versions.

Nichol's typographical poems range from the simple (in *Still Water*) to the complex (in *bp*). *Still Water* is composed of poems that require only a single glance to produce their full impression. The opening poem sets the playful tone: "two leaves touch/ bad poems are written." On one page the word "star" is reproduced as "st*r" while on another page the word "empty" is rewritten "em ty." Similarly, "grow" receives an additional "w" — becoming "groww". Other poems include "closedpen" and "waiting" followed

o   pen

by a blank page. What saves *Still Water* from banality is its brilliant physical production. The book is a five-inch square flip-top box; the outside cover is a sheet of shimmering reflective foil with the words "Still Water" centrally printed in black. Inside, each poem is on a separate unbending piece of very high quality white paper,

127

and requires the reader's active participation to turn the pages. Overall, the excellent design of the book leads me to accept the light-hearted nature of *Still Water*, and to demand no more of the poems than a quick smile.

Nichol's small press, Ganglia, and its arms — grOnk, Synapsis, Tonto or Series, Singing Hand Series, 5¢ series, and 35¢ Mimeo Series — have put out many of his ephemeral pieces of poetry. For instance, *Final Concrete Testament* is a very thin, small piece of paper folded over once. The title appears on the outside and, like a greeting card, on the inside appears one word — "dead". *A Condensed History of Nothing* is slightly larger than *Concrete Testament*, having three small pieces of paper folded over. There is nothing written or marked on the inside pages. *a little pome for yur fingertips* is printed on three high quality pieces of small sized white paper. The words of the title and the inside pages are impressed on the page, because the reader is supposed to use his "fingertips" not his eyes. The words are: "love, lovely, loAve, A lover." This was printed by "Tonto or 4" in a run of thirty copies.

While some observers believe that concrete poetry can be dated no earlier than 1954,[4] Nichol thinks that concrete poetry has "been around too many years to mention   just open your favourite occult book at any page of diagrams   there it is   flip to the coloured comics on a saturday."[5] In an interview, Nichol describes concrete poetry as "the working with visual rhythms, with words I guess, much the way a painter would. It's taking language and dealing with the smallest particle of information, say the letters."[6]

For Nichol the history of concrete poetry stretches back to Greek (400 B.C.) and, later, to Christian pattern poems (500 A.D.). His "Christian Cross #2" (Fig. 1) recreates one of the basic visual shapes of the Greeks and Christians — the cross — but in a contemporary light. Only one word, "theory", is used, but the contrasting italics set out the interior words — "the", "or", and "y". Read together, these three words ask a pertinent question: "the" (an article used as a nominal) is the church laws; "or" is or; and "y" is "why?". To paraphrase, the question reads: should church laws be accepted without dispute? Note also that the word "theory," which provides the building blocks for the cross pattern, semantically represents the foundation of the church.[7] The ability to create such poetic compression must be viewed as one of Nichol's chief assets.

```
    theory
    theory
    theory
theory theory theory
theory theory theory
theory theory theory
    theory
    theory
    theory
    theory
    theory
    theory
```

Fig. 1

In *Konfessions of an Elizabethan Fan Dancer*, the typewriter and the mimeograph provide the tools that determine the appearance of the poems. *Konfessions*, Nichol's largest collection of typewriter poems, demonstrates what he terms "the typewriter's tremendous advantage — that each character occupies exactly the same space as any other character." Accordingly, "the most successful poems . . . are those which acknowledge and work with this fact," as well as those that explore semantical patterns. The least successful typewriter poems are those which tend "toward typographical decorativeness and simply typewriter games."[8]

Nichol's typewriter poetry often suffers by his own evaluatory criteria — that is, it has extreme simplicity of shape or meaning or else relies too heavily on a trick. Many of the typewriter poems in *Konfessions* are at about the same level of density as those in *Still Water*. "pan/rain/pain/" or "Counting the Ways" ("love" repeated seven times like an addition question yielding "llove") are representative example from *Konfessions*. As Nichol himself observes, "the pun is in danger of getting overused in

129

concrete   not enough poets realize the skill needed to handle it effectively." Of the twenty-nine poems in *Konfessions* (first edition only), eight are visual notations of sound poems (which I shall discuss later); a few are permutational poems, as when "pulpits" and "tulips" exchange position; several are typewriter designs, without semantic content; and two — "The End of the Affair" and "blues" — are clearly superior to the rest.

"The End of the Affair" (Fig. 2) is significant for two separate reasons: first, it is one of Nichol's more successful typewriter poems; second, it clarifies Nichol's creative process. In John Robert Colombo's anthology *How Do I Love Thee*, Nichol writes that he chose "The End of the Affair" for his favourite poem because the writing of the poem drove away "the bummer" and "thru this poem i crystallized a state of mind, . . . and thru that crystallization re-entered the flow of my life" (p. 160).

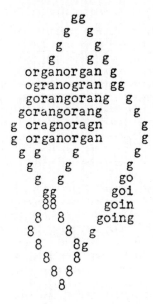

Fig. 2

The poem is based on three adjacent parallelograms of "g" 's and one of "8" 's. Overlaying the "g" 's are the letters "o,r,a,n" creating the words "organ", "o gran", and "go ran or go rang". The title directs the reading of the poem, and emphasizes the words "organ" (sexual affair) and "go" "ran" (movement or escape).

The "g" 's turn into "8" 's at the bottom of the page; on their sides the "8" 's are symbols (∞) for infinity; and for Nichol, "infinite was the key word" in the poem. The shift in meaning triggers the physical shift of "g go goi goin going" and consequently the "end of the affair." The rigidity of typewritten spacing combines with the similar shapes of "g" and "8" and "∞" to reinforce the patterned constricting feeling in the poem.

In the covering remarks to his poem in *How Do I Love Thee*, Nichol makes some remarks on his compositional process. He says that he did not select the actual poem but rather selected "the voice (that) spoke thru me that day (since many speak thru me many different ways)". He views the writing process as completely dependent on the writer's physical make-up at the moment of writing. In a similar vein, Nichol said that he couldn't revise one of his older manuscripts because "i am no longer the person i was when i wrote these. my musculature is different and (as a result) my breathing."[9] In *The Martyrology* (Book II) he noted that "i throw up these poems/ out of the *moment* of the soul's searching / part of the process of gaining focus" (my emphasis). Focus and crystallization, then, are his goals; and each time he writes, his breath and musculature impose different results on the style of the poem. In other words, he regards poetry as being totally integrated with life:

the poem begins and ends nowhere
being part of the flow you live with
starts when you're born
stepping in and out of
such moments you are aware
emerge as pages put in a book and titled
                    (*The Other Side of the Room*)

131

In the other excellent poem, "blues" (Fig. 3), Nichol displays the word "love" in a geometrical grid together with its reverse spelling — "evol". Thus the typographical precision predicates the necessary relationship between "love" and "evol". In *The Captain Poetry Poems*, however, Nichol warns that "evol/ is nature's way (i've/ overworked it/ in a dozen (poems) has/ nothing to do/ with evil but rather evolves/ new themes." The correlation, therefore, is meant to be between love and evolution, not love and evil.[10]

```
    l  e
      o e
    love
    o evol
love o
    evol
  e o
  e l
```

Fig. 3

Besides typewriter poems, Nichol has widely experimented with typographical poems. In *ABC: The Aleph Beth Book* Nichol examines each letter of the alphabet and designs with them and around them. He refers to the letters as "tight imagistic things intended for what they teach the eye on one looking, . . . not meant as pictures but as syllabic and sub-syllabic messages for those who care to listen."[11] These messages are "primarily concerned with getting below language to those things Sapir referred to as forming 'the actual life of language' " which includes the "unarticulated content of signs."[12]

Interwoven with these alphabetic signs in *ABC* is a message declaring that "poetry is dead" and that to revivify it, the poet must break through the traditional barriers of language. This polemic is printed in full at the opening of *ABC*, then reprinted fragment by fragment on each of the twenty-six pages, and again, fully, on the final page. The exploration of the single letter, the book implies, is one possible way to recreate the life in poetry.

Nichol's most complex and well-crafted collection of

132

typographical poems is contained in *bp*. Thanks to the excellent printing job done by Stan Bevington in conjunction with Nichol, these poems stand out both individually and as a group. In "owl", the four letters "o,w,l, and h" are printed in a variety of type faces, colours, and combinations on the bold orange postcard sized piece of heavy paper. Some of the phrases created include: "low owl, how o owl, how o low, who owl, howl owl". "Mind Trap" looks like a non-linear Habitat. Within its construction, various letters of the alphabet can be distinguished, including: L, E, F, T, D, H, and I. Thus the trap, besides being a physical maze, is also a language prison that prevents letters from gaining liberation.

Although sound poetry is sometimes referred to as a separate genre from concrete poetry, it can also be viewed as a subdivision of concrete poetry because of its concentration on and exploitation of language possibilities. Whereas in typographical poems the shape of the letters and the space on the page draw poetic attention, in sound poetry it is the sound of words and letters that is explored. In reviewing Bill Bissett's *The Jinx Ship Nd Othr Trips*, Nichol pays tribute to Bissett who stimulated Nichol's initial "concrete explorations in '63 after encounters with Dada and the writings of Bill Bissett" (Geddes, p. 590). In both Bissett's and Nichol's sound poetry "the poem is a written score only in so much as it gives him the basic words or sounds to be followed. The rest is improvisation on his part in which he varies the tone, the emphasis, the phrasing, the speed, etc."

Nichol's attempt to relate the sound poem and its written text is representative of his larger struggle with poetic form in general. Thus it will prove worthwhile to examine in detail his varying methods of printing sound texts, beginning with "Cycle #22" (Fig. 4). It is one of Nichol's earliest sound poems and starts with the four words "drum anda wheel anda." When the "w" of "wheel" becomes attached to the previous word "anda" creating "wandaw", the pattern is initiated that runs the length of the poem. Every third word picks up the lead letter of the following word, as can be seen by tracing the diagonals from left-top to right-bottom of each word. By line eighteen the original line is restored. Nichol's reading of "Cycle #22" (on *Borders* in *bp*) places the emphasis on "drum" and "wheel" and their alterations from lines 1-7 and from lines 11-18. The middle lines are varied, with stress on "dadr" which is pronounced like "dada." The overall effect of "Cycle #22" is, as the title suggests, cyclical.

Like "Cycle #22", "Dada Lama" has a written text which corresponds to the sound composition. At one time, Nichol "used to write out the texts wringing a formal number of semantic or phonetic changes and perform the piece according to that set text."[13] Unlike "Cycle #22" 's words, the sounds in "Dada Lama" are translated as letters. For example, the opening four lines are: "hweeeee/ hweeeee/ hyonnnn/ hyonnnn." If the reader has not heard Nichol chanting "Dada Lama" then he cannot imagine the donkey-like way these combinations are voiced.

From this simple attempt, Nichol progressed to the complicated notational system used in *Scraptures: 5th Sequence*. There are sixteen separate techniques employed, most of which are electronic (tape fade-outs) and some of which are human (tongue-clicking sounds). This process is further described in Nichol's article, "From Sound to Sense".

```
drum anda wheel
anda drum andaw
heel anda druma
ndaw heel andad
ruma ndaw heela
ndad ruma ndawh
eela ndad ruman
dawh eela ndadr
uman dawh eelan
dadr uman dawhe
elan dadr umand
awhe elan dadru
mand awhe eland
adru mand awhee
land adru manda
```

```
whee land adrum
anda whee landa
drum anda wheel
```

Fig. 4

Eventually, dissatisfaction with the complexities led him, he says, to eliminate virtually any notational system and rather to carry the systems around in his head. "carnage ikawa is th entire *print* text of a poem called Hiroshima (mon amour) which lasts anywhere from 3 to 6 minutes." At present, Nichol relies on his own "psychological response and the audience's physiological response" to determine how a poem like "Hiroshima" is to be read at any particular time and place.

The problem took on a new dimension when more voices were added. In 1970, Nichol and Steve McCaffery gave a joint poetry reading in Toronto. Later, joined by Rafael Barreto-Rivera and Paul Dutton, they named themselves the Four Horsemen and began giving group readings. Their system of notations, says Nichol, "evolved . . . simply to let ourselves know at which point our voices come together, at which point they follow different courses." In the summer of 1971, the Four Horsemen became interested in musical instruments as voice extensions, one result being "michael drayton".[14] A year later, they decided to cease using musical instruments in order to "return poetry to its origin, the human voice, and away from the printed page."[15]

A more recent example of the Four Horsemen's notational system is "Poem #1" (Fig. 5). Note that the numbers 1-4 stand for each poet, and that time is blocked out in unspecified units. Even this system, however, has proved too cumbersome "since the notational system (like any language) limits your thinking." Accordingly they have opted towards "a more spheroid (i.e. non-linear) means of notating." Nichol's practice of marking down the sounds has moved from simple (in "Dada Lama") to complex (in *Scraptures:5th Sequence*), back to simple ("in Poem #1"), and finally to "non-linear". Appropriately, such a difficulty and such a solution characterize Nichol's poetic; in this case, as in typographical poems (and later, as we shall see, in his prose), Nichol feels limited by traditional, linear, sequential, ideational language and has to adopt bold new alternatives to express his inspirations. One such option exists through the power of sound poetry to "heal the split that has become more and more apparent since the invention of the printing press."

Nichol arbitrarily draws the distinction between his prose and his poetry. He uses "prose" in the title of *Nights on Prose Mountain*, probably because the shape of the words on the page more resembles what is thought of as prose. However, the opening paragraph from "a little preface" in *Nights on Prose Mountain* could equally be classified as one or the other. "a tiny blue, a green, eastern and western, certain possible things, magic in the guise of scince. Shaman." The periods function like end-line breaks; they stop the reading for a brief pause. Later variations of this paragraph occur: "a tiny green, a blue, we talked of personal things. . . . an eastern green. a western blue."

In "a little preface" to *Nights on Prose Mountain* Nichol mentions the "personal saints" — saint ranglehold, saint reat, saint agnes, saint and. Nichol pronounces the saints in full, i.e. "Saint And", but they are also meant to be seen as their contractions St. And or stand, St. Ranglehold or stranglehold. Together with a long list of other saints, these saints form the basis for *The Martyrology*. In his introduction to *The Martyrology*, Nichol sees himself "standing awkwardly at the entrance to their shrine" with hat in hand. At that time, he believed that "all the words ... were saints (language the holy place of consecraton." But towards the end of *Book II*, he viewed language as "the prototype/ perfect model of the robot run amuck." What matters now is to "return again to human voice and listen / rip off the mask of words to free the sounds."

The central theme of *The Martyrology: Books I-II* is language and the poetic process. Overall there is a double concern: to discuss poetry while at the same time to incorporate these poetical theories into the poem itself. It is Nichol writing about writing, "because the basic material

		rows		risen	risen	rising	sing	arise
rose	roses	arise			rising	rising	ing	arisen
	a rose is	a rose is			rising	rising	ring	arisen
		roses	arise			risen	ing	arisen

Fig. 5

of all literature IS language." Examining himself and his writing, he thinks that "everything i say / i have said before / once when i thot each phrase new / and now see the mockery of speech." The obstacle to achieving some kind of human freedom is writing itself: "if i could throw down this pen i never use / then i could live my life free of naming." Another reason not to write is that there might not be "adequate words to fit the mind's / conceptions." Nichol's "way of reaching" towards truth is to turn "backwards into the mind." In that land, "there is a peace the mind can breathe in / nothing but the tangles in my tongue / let sounds sweep in around me / in a heaven with no need of poetry." At the end of *Book II*, Nichol comes to some tentative conclusions: "she is right you know saint rand / stein did say / the hardest thing is making the present continuous / living day to day." Writing day to day in the continuing present is the crucial obstacle to Nichol, because writing is the key that unlocks doors to unknown places: "only the words you trust to take you thru to what place you don't know." How you reach this goal is in

turning back
taking what you've found and turning it outward
    into the world   its really that simple
i suppose no one ever knew
that   last door will open st rand
if you really want it to

Andy is Nichol's most satisfying long prose work as well as being one of the most original and exciting works written in Canada. It is a collage of five sections which intertwine and eventually coalesce. The first section is made up of correspondence from Andy to Barrie which describes Andy's stay in Paris. These letters are familiar in style and full of local gossip. At first printed in full, after a few pages the letters appear as fragments without date, addressee, or addressor. The second section is written in a pseudo-scientific, futuristic style; it is ostensibly concerned with travel, but this only serves as a metaphor to explore the movement of language from ideational to emotional. Next is a melodramatic Doctor-Nurse story about heart transplants and the worship of the Nurse for the Doctor. The fourth story is explicitly pornographic and details the sexual activities of Rory and Sophia. Finally there is a narrative, in the form of a diary and letters, describing a journey through the Korenski mountains into a hidden valley where a great civilization of the past once lived.

As with any art form that uses collage or juxtaposition as its major stylistic device, in *Andy* the relationship at the interfaces of any two separate sections is of much interest. At one point, the explorers' guide Yaboo gets frostbite, but bravely continues to work. "Have to admire the man's courage," says the explorer in his diary. The next sentence begins one line lower, but at the same horizontal position. "holding holding control will you please give me a reading on probable limitation of present track." The shift from Yaboo's courage to airplane communication jargon creates a semantical overlap on "probably limitation" of Yaboo in his "present" condition. Then, the next shift: "He felt her tongue on his balls and pressed his crotch into her face." Here the words "holding holding:" carry a double responsibility. Next: "we just put up one big tent last night and huddled together for warmth." The explorer's story again, but this time the overtones of "big tent" and "huddled together for warmth" are controlled by the sexual description. We are returned to the pilot's dilemma. "control? control? do you still read me? conjunctions

138

noted as frequently occurring." Who is in control? Rory? The explorers? Very cleverly, Nichol has punned on "do you read me?" and asks the question of the book's reader — Is the reader in control? And so it goes from section to section — great amounts of meaning overlapping from ingenious juxtapositions.

Two reviewers of *Andy*, Matt Cohen and Pat Bates, have thought that *everything* was written by Andy's persona.[16] Bates posits that the letters from Andy are "somewhat like commercials interspread between his many mad movie imaginings." Internal evidence for this position is rather slim. In Andy's opening letter he signs off with: "So we'll be seeing you shortly and I'll be telling you miles of nonsense then." In his final letter he says: "You know Bar I'm a very funny character. I'm living fantasies all the time. I've fucked about 10-18 girls in my fantasies and not one in reality." Other than these fragments describing Andy's penchant for fantasy, the only other reason for considering this to be completely a creation of Andy's imagination is the title itself, *Andy*, which serves as a clue to the author's conception of the book.

Whether or not (and I think not)[17] Andy's persona wrote the whole book, the aspect of *Andy* most consistent with all of Nichol's works is the opposition to traditional language forms. This opposition is crystallized in the pseudo-scientific "Mission Control" sections, parts of which, according to Matt Cohen, are incomprehensible and create "a nice impression of electronic verbiage." "Mission Control" allows Nichol to enter his own thoughts about the writing of the book into the book: "too much cleverness, the probably death of a third attempt. two rough drafts now discarded." This double effect of the author discussing the work in progress includes redirecting the "focus movement outward from word to flow. repetitive death of linear emotion. spheroid emotional state now in ascendancy." All the effort of the book is aimed at the "reversal of linear sequential thinking." We have seen how Nichol attacks this problem in concrete poetry by getting back to the roots of language; "now the problem i'm at this point is that now I want to get ideas in."[18]

139

How to do this? "I have to go on to whole new forms." As described at the beginning of *Andy*, the book is "fragments of incomplete. the whole thing welded as it were ungainly." These descriptions, of course, are not totally coherent in any grammatical sense but the meaning is clear: incomplete fragments are ungainly welded. When the new form is achieved, it is concurrently described: "moving into union of matter. moving into mattering union." The union of matter results from the intertwining of the five collage sections; mattering union occurs because of the common semantical direction of these sections. All five sections describe searching; the Dr. — nurse story searches for the way to put the heart back into the patient (read: the emotion back into language); the explorer searches for the lost civilization through innumerable caves (entrances and exits); Rory seeks the "deepest penetration at end of sexual act" in order to achieve female orgasm (the emotional union of male and female which cannot co-exist with the ideational union); and Andy seeks Barrie as a way to understand himself (to discover what he "wants to say" and to ask "many questions").

The physical book itself (the first edition only) forces the reader to reexamine his sense of what writing means. *Andy* starts at the back and moves towards the front. *For Jesus Lunatick*, the other of the *Two Novels*, starts in the middle but is upside down compared to *Andy*. As well, the drawings are separate from the text and are to be cut and glued to their appropriately numbered position. These unexpected circumstances combine with the words into a "union of matter. a mattering union" one step removed from, but in rhythm with, the stylistic devices of *Andy*.

If it is not blasphemy to categorize Nichol, I think three broad labels can be attached to him and his writings. First, he is an idealist in his belief that a "new humanism will one day touch the world to its core." He believes that love and evolution work jointly to bring on this new humanism. Second, Nichol is a traditionalist; "it is necessary if we are to continue fruitfully that we open our eyes and ears once more to that non-productive tradition."[19] In other words, "traditional poetry is only one of the means by which to reach out and touch the other." Third, he is a radical writer, digging back to the auditory and visual roots to bring new life into the language.

i suppose if i have a general theme its the language trap and that runs thru the centre of everything i do. style is disregarded in favor of reproduction of actual states of mind in order to follow these states thru the particular traps they become in search of possible exits. hence for me there is no discrepancy to pass back and forth between trad poetry, concrete poetry, sound poetry, film, comic strips, the novel or what have you in order to reproduce the muse that musses up my own brain.[20]

Figures

¹ Edward Sapir, "Language," as quoted by Nichol in "Review of 'The Jinx Ship Nd Othr Trips'," Quarry, 16 (1967), 43.

² William Carlos Williams as quoted by Nichol in "The Typography of Bill Bissett," in Bill Bissett's *We Sleep Inside Each Othr All* (Toronto: Ganglia Press, 1966), n. pag.

³ Nichol, "Statement," in *bp* (Toronto: Coach House Press, 1967), n. pag.

⁴ See, for instance, Eugen Gomringer, "The First Years of Concrete Poetry," *Form*, 4 (April, 1967), 17-18.

⁵ In *The Cosmic Chef: An Evening of Concrete*, ed. bpNichol (Ottawa: Oberon Press, 1970), p. 64.

⁶ George Bowering, "Cutting Them All Up: An Interview with BP Nichol," *Alphabet*, 18/19 (1971), 18.

⁷ Nichol writes, in a letter to the author, September, 1974, "the other thing i consciously worked with was the the or and (y being Spanish for the conjunction that rules our life) but i'm sure you know all that stuff about the specific versus the dualistic".

⁸ Nichol, "Review of 'Typewriter Poems'," *Open Letter*, 3 (2nd series) (Fall, 1972), 79.

⁹ Nichol, *Beach Head* (Sacramento: Runcible Spoon, 1970), n. pag.

¹⁰ Nichol letter, September 1974, " 'nature's way' is a quote from the old SERUTAN ads 'REMEMBER! Serutan is natures spelt backwards!' "

¹¹ Nichol in *An Anthology of Concrete Poetry*, ed. Emmett Williams, (New York: Something Else Press, 1967), p. 224.

¹² Nichol in *20th Century Poetry and Poetics*, ed. Gary Geddes, (Toronto: Oxford, 1970), p. 590.

¹³ Nichol, "From Sound to Sense," *Stereo Headphones*, 4 (Spring, 1971), n. pag.

¹⁴ Recorded on *Canadada*, (Toronto: Griffin House, 1971).

¹⁵ Rafael Barreto-Rivera on the liner notes to *Canadada*.

¹⁶ Matt Cohen, "Slickly Sensuous," *Saturday Night*, 85 (June, 1970), 35; Pat Martin Bates, "Two 'Lautgedichte' singers: Victor Coleman and bp nichol," *Arts/Canada*, 27 (April, 1970), 65.

¹⁷ Nichol letter, September 1974, "you're right the letters in *Andy* are actual letters from Andy Phillips (my dear friend & brother of my dear friend David Phillips (the David of THE MARTYROLOGY))".

¹⁸ Bowering interview, 19.

¹⁹ Nichol, "Letter re James Reaney," *Open Letter*, 6 (2nd series) (Fall, 1973), 6.

²⁰ Nichol quoted in *Contemporary Poets of the English Language*, ed. Rosalie Murphy, (Chicago & London: St. James Press, 1970), p. 798.

bill bissett / Poetics, Politics & Vision

Len Early

"Frivolity and ecstasy are the twin poles between which play moves." (Johan Huizinga, *Homo Ludens*)

In some three dozen books of poetry published since 1966, bill bissett has often seemed intent on making a virtue of disorder. If the redundancy of much of his work is undeniable, so is its great variety. Challenging all manner of authority, literary and otherwise, he has mounted an attack on convention that at times appears nihilistic to the point of stunting his considerable artistry. Nevertheless, there is a vital consistency in his theories, forms and themes. The most idiosyncratic and the most ideological of his poems reveal a visionary writer whose achievement is already an impressive one.

While bissett's poetic is fairly obvious in many of his volumes, two are expressly addressed to questions of language and style: *Rush / What Fuckan Theory* (1971) and *Words in th Fire* (1972). The first of these is a book subverted by its own attitudes. As an assertion of bissett's idea that relationships such as hierarchy, cause-effect sequences, and linear writing are repressive, *Rush* proclaims its defiance by remaining determinedly incoherent. The verbal chaos is extreme; only occasionally are there passages of striking intellectual or lyrical interest.

Almost all the important points in bissett's aesthetic view which are diffused, obscured and repeated elsewhere in the book, are tellingly concentrated in one poem, "Poetry dusint have to be," which presents some of his most persistent themes. He declares that poetry should be free from any prescriptions of subject; indeed, like the most elementary child's play, it can do "nothing well." Nevertheless, as the bulk of this manifesto demonstrates, poetry can very well be about political and social issues of the utmost consequence — and much of bissett's own work is. The idea that there is a close connection between rules of language and political oppression (one of bissett's central convictions) occurs in the third part of the poem, and in the fourth he touches on another of his main themes: life in a primitive, natural terrain. In conclusion he suggests that the poet may be a medium for the utterance of perceptions which elude his conscious understanding:

> writing pomes can be abt many things
> can be abt nothing but what it itself is
> writing pomes in a way is longr than we are
> and what we can know writing pomes
> is also th voice uv ths things speaking thru us

"Poetry dusint have to be" is typical in form of those of bissett's poems which develop as predominantly discursive works, as distinguished from the visceral chants and visual designs at which he also excels. While he eschews conventional grammar and punctuation in such poems, they give an impression of copious vitality, of perceptions rendered articulate through the rhythms of phrase, line and section — or as bissett would have it, through the rhythms of breath.

Words in th Fire (1972) uses this discursive mode to develop "anothr/ study uv langwage" with much greater lucidity that *Rush*. In this series of semi-continuous meditations, bissett sees himself as participating in a "langwage revolution" which, however, appears to him to be faltering at the time he writes this poem. One aspect of this revolution, he suggests, is the wide availability of

144

typewriters, copiers, small presses — a cultural phenomenon which subverts authority systems. Among bissett's ideals is that of an organic principle in poetic structures. This notion is hardly revolutionary, unless we extend the history of the revolution back at least as far as Wordsworth and Coleridge. However, the radical practices of bissett and some of his contemporaries are almost unprecedented. While the history of twentieth-century poetry is in large part an account of the revolt against nineteenth-century stanzas, rhythm and rhyme schemes, concrete poets in our time have carried the revolt further, in their suspicion of basic semantic conventions like grammar, spelling and linear printing, which they regard as repressive systems. bissett stresses the importance in his kind of poetry, of *sound*, especially of language as spoken, as opposed to language as it is taught in schools. He seeks to present:

> that vois ther on th page moving along into that
> nd it skips yes it stops yes it pauses cheks yu out to see if yr
> > gettin it right
> > all that so it dont
> > on th page vizually stay
> in square blocks

bissett's "revolutionary" spelling is conceived as a political act, intended to embody the values of phonetic simplification and vocal authenticity. "Correct" expression is in his view elitist, one more self-perpetuating device of the privileged classes, and one more restriction on the creative spirit. The anatomy of his books reflects this attitude: variations in the size of pages, inserts of advertisements and items clipped from magazines and newspapers, crayon drawings, inverted pages, pages of different colors — chiefly pastels in green, pink, grey, and blue, print that ranges from pica type to Olde English lettering, hand-written poems — his methods of defying standardization seem inexhaustible.

bissett praises the potential of poetry to stir our faculties and involve readers in something akin to the act of poetic creation, an experience directly in contrast to the chief "recreation" of our age, television, which is generally manipulative rather than stimulating. Or as bissett himself says with more point, in "radiashun collaps":

cant watch tv no mor man
ths tv's gotta go or me go
cant watch it baby how cum
it needs to be watchd
all th time   cant lord
cant no way lord ths tv
just a pile of shit

(in *Th High Green Hill*)

This is not to say that bissett is unaware of the power of words to deceive and subjugate. His enthusiasm for language as delight, as freedom, as discovery, is equalled by his suspicion of language as an instrument of tyranny. As early as *The Jinx Ship nd Othr Trips* (1966), he is quite clear about the power of language to constrict and damage our lives. Fundamental to bissett's work is his conviction that because poetry issues from minds which are continually conditioned by their environment, any view of poetry must take account of the social, the political, indeed the *physical* milieu in which it emerges. Hence *Words in th Fire* includes passages on the urbanization of modern consciousness, on discrimination against Canadian poets, the inequities of book distribution, Canadian complicity in the war in Vietnam, and on the Americanization of Canada. For bissett, political empire is intimately associated with language and thought control. Similarly, literary criticism is a form of power politics: "tastes get stratified nd start to stand for/ what is permitted to get thru."

In the interest of "liberating" language from traditional poetic forms, bissett has explored its visual and aural qualities: the former is the route to concrete poetry, the latter leads to sound poetry. An extremely protean phenomenon, concrete poetry is hard to define with any precision: generally, it exploits the strictly visual properties of words while making more or less use of their semantic content. I think that bissett's "am or," from

146

Awake in th Red Desert (1968), is a paradigm of concrete. Semantically, "am" expresses the fundamental human condition of isolated subjectivity, and "or" raises the question of an alternative state: can one's loneliness be eased? Yes, in fact the solution to human isolation is love: "amor." And the culmination of love is reached at the end of the poem in the form of sexual communion popularly known as "sixty-nine." Visually, the stark columns of "ams" and "ors" may suggest the monotonous isolation of two individuals. The fact that these columns merge into the cluster of "69's" and the fact that in contrast to the columns, most of the "69's" are linked, reinforces my "semantic" reading. The 69's are also a clue to another visual dimension of the poem. If one inverts the page, the phallic shape becomes instantly apparent, accounting for the notch at the top of the figure. Righting the page, we now perceive the figure as a female emblem as well. (The fact that the shape of the poem is male upside down and female rightside up, corresponds to the physical positions of the lovers as they engage in "sixty-nine.") This is at once a love poem and an erotic sketch, altogether a work of considerable cleverness and perhaps of some emotional value, as far as it touches our own sense of loneliness and our knowledge or our hope of love.

The variety of bissett's concrete poems continually challenges his readers' abilities to respond to the unusual. In "am or," the visual and semantic elements are almost in balance. As the proportion of semantic content in concrete poetry diminishes, the form approaches that of the purely visual arts — indeed, bissett is a graphic artist of considerable talent. One of his favorite methods is collage. Towards the end of the *Pass th Food Release th Spirit Book* (1973), we come upon a page on which a panel evidently clipped from a comic book is placed amid four snapshots arranged to form a frame and background. The cartoon depicts two girls fleeing on horseback from a looming tyrannosaurus which has just emerged from the jungle. Each of the photographs shows a modern high-rise office or apartment building. The only words in the collage are those of one of the girls, whose speech-balloon says,

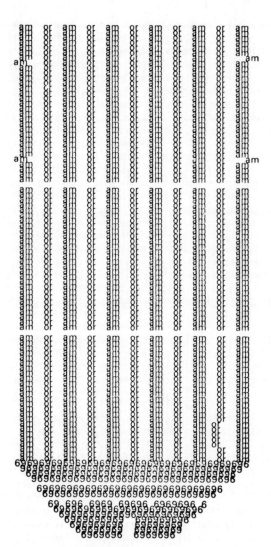

"Go, Samie!" (We can't be sure whether she's addressing her horse or the other girl.) Commentary: the collage invites a comparison of the tyrannosaurus with the rampant high-rises of our concrete jungles, modern monsters which threaten to devour us. The monstrous qualities of the high-rises — their dehumanized geometry and the standardized compartments (apart/ments) into which they separate people, are suggested by contrast. In the photographs only a solitary human figure appears, so tiny as to be nearly imperceptible, dwarfed at the entrance to his building; the comic strip, however, is vivid with creatures and companions as well as with terror. The whole effect is deliberately hokey, but nevertheless makes a point about the tyranny wrought by technologized environments. Such work can also remind us that the conceptual content of concrete poetry is not contingent on its semantic content. The pictorial symbols and many of the figures in bissett's drawings are full of meaning, and often enrich and complement the themes of his more traditional poems.

One obvious way to reduce the semantic content of a concrete poem is to keep the words to a minimum. Another way is to repeat a particular word or group of words until our sense of their conceptual meaning disappears. This is a primary technique of sound poetry but it also has a function in printed works. In a poem from *What* (1974), as the semantic import of the word evaporates, our attention is attracted by its concrete properties — the shapes and patterns of letters:

                    what
              what   what
                    what
              what   what
                    what
              what   what
                    what
              what   what
                    what
              what   what
                    what

Traditional writing tends to abstract us from the phenomenal world; a number of bissett's concrete poems seek to
reverse this tendency by insisting on the shapes and
spaces of print and of calligraphy.

Like conventional poetry, concrete ranges from the
utterly simple to the highly complex, from merely formal
designs which can be appreciated at a glance, to collages
of words and shapes which yield sophisticated meanings.
And like conventional poetry, it ranges from the lightest,
most sportive poems, to works of profound moral import.
The former seems to be more generally the case: more
often concrete poetry amuses and delights than it informs
and instructs. It would be more faithful to the spirit of the
genre to dispense with the critical term "work" and to
speak of art*play*. bissett's *What Poetiks* (1967) is a series of
childish scrawls, bad jokes, elementary puns — a treatment of language as simple visual and semantic counters.
*IBM / Saga uv th Relees uv Human Spirit from Compuew-
terr Funckshuns* (no date) plays concrete games with the
alphabet, chiefly through discerning pictures in the
shapes of letters, and through word association. *What*
(1974) is a brown envelope containing loose pages which
can be shuffled into any sequence. Among the poems is
"vowl man," a human figure constructed of a's, e's, i's, o's
and u's. Other pages present more or less recognizable
shapes built out of numerous "what's" — there are a
building, a table, a barbecue and I *think* a handsaw. There
are a couple of dim photographs of what appears to be
lovemaking, and there is an introductory poem which
needn't, naturally, appear at the beginning of the sequence. The title word is a brilliant stroke. As a query,
"what" expresses precisely our attitude as we encounter
each poem; as an assertion, it quite rightly indicates that
each poem is no more nor less than itself. What? what.
That's what.

As does concrete, sound poetry moves from relatively
familiar uses of language (recitation, song), to works
devoid of conceptual meaning: wails, hums and chants in
which the voice is used strictly as an instrument of sound,
speaking only to our emotions, not at all to our intellect.

The most satisfactory experience of bissett's sound poetry is, of course, a live performance by the man himself. Listening to bissett on a record player or tape deck is similar to watching a rock concert on television: one feels that the performance is unnaturally packaged and controlled, and misses a vital sense of immediacy and of communal experience. Very little of bissett's sound poetry eschews the semantic element altogether, though most of his auditors will respond to only sound qualities in those chants ("shun da kalensha ta da lee") which are, according to Frank Davey, "based on west coast Indian material."[1] "Take th river into yr heart," is a typical section of bissett's chant, "Th water falls in yr mind nd yu get wet tooo," which is printed in *Liberating Skies* (1969), and recorded on the LP that accompanies *Medicine My Mouth's on Fire* (1974). Perhaps the line can be understood in several ways, but it is certainly an exhortation to transcend oneself. The repetition which characterizes bissett's chanting frequently acquires ritual and sacramental overtones; indeed, much of his sound poetry ultimately amounts to a religious use of language and is closely related to the sacred vision which surges through such volumes as *Polar Bear Hunt* (1972) and *Th High Green Hill* (1972). As it is chanted, the line undergoes a variety of spontaneous vocal modulations. Its printed version can illustrate another facet of bissett's sound poetry: the typewritten "notation" for the work renders a concrete poem of considerable visual beauty. Such "tapestries" of words approach another of bissett's art forms: designs created by the typewriter which have no cognitive meaning, and whose charms are purely visual.

Often the puzzling forms which bissett's work takes have the effect of slowing down our experience of the poetry. Perhaps this is one of the fundamental virtues of his technique: it forces us to assume a more leisurely pace, to enter into the spirit of play, of reverence, of creation itself; it resists the "expert" response of programmed analysis and cataloguing. Indeed a number of concrete poets have stated that a primary aim of their work is involvement of the reader in completing or contributing to the poem's meaning in much greater measure than conventional poetry demands. Thus Claus Bremer, in an explanation of one of his poems: "this arrangement is intended to arouse curiosity, to reveal something, and then again to become obscure; to arouse the reader's curiosity, to reveal something to him, and then again confront him with himself. . . . Concrete poetry gives us no results. It yields a process of discovery. It is motion. Its motion ends in different readers in different ways."[2] Much of bissett's work is intriguing in this way and gratifies our efforts to appreciate it.

There are, however, numerous poems and passages throughout the spate of volumes by bissett, which for me lack any aesthetic merit. In poems such as "run tonight" from *Pass th Food Release th Spirit Book* (1973), I can find neither the exuberance nor the beauty which are outstanding qualities elsewhere in his work. I remarked that as a revolutionary writer, bissett seeks to shatter the conventional orders of language, and that some of his most vital work is a consequence of this enterprise. Poems like "run

```
run   tonight   and i ull
use yur assa im poemd well
lots of wanta sure have they
look              like
yu                 th
cud          white one in
have        our stomachs
a            i im just   yank
pressed     it du yu
book              hees gone   to
isint             jiggul   him self
that              must have atnos
xcitin            hair   he married
                            all those flowers
yu see        all kinds f things     thats what togo r
it            for i cin smell      going   stop
   wud         hasint                       nd
very be                    swept          one
    good      this room                   heel
for          it even he sat on              south
  blind      that where i cud have found   nd
  peopul     mail nd                            mirrors
       its here this time it well there was no    in th back
                                  one            as
                                        these webs
                                      ahaaha
                                      these nd
                                      th bay
                                    pardon
                                    belonged
                                         to
                                         us
                                          wild
                                  fuckan things
```

tonight," though, strike me as applications of his theories about language rather than explorations of the medium itself.

This self-conscious effect is reminiscent of Dada and surrealist art; indeed many of bissett's poems which baffle attempts to "read" them, echo the Dada interest, noted by Nahma Sandrow, in "dissociation and negation, in mocking with obscene gestures society and intellect and art, all illusions of an era too pigheaded to confront its chaos."[3] In "run tonight," disordered structure and violation of coherence are themselves the point. While such work may have a purpose of sorts, it fails to realize the aesthetic possibilities of either concrete or "trad" poetry. It has neither formal nor intellectual appeal, and seems to me essentially the printed equivalent of noise. Too often one feels that bissett is merely giving the raspberry to an especially pedantic fifth-rate English teacher he may have encountered in grammar school. It's worth noting that bissett himself is quite willing to make judgements about the quality of his poetry. Though he frequently urges us to let things, and poems, "be themselves," he acknowledges in a preface to *Sunday Work* (1969) that "sum uv ths pomes aren't ordinarily worth publishing or writing," and the volume *Living with th Vishyun* (1974) begins with this invitation:


```
        ar
    sum     uv ths
  pomes      bul
   shit       see if
   yu can tell
     wch ar
          sum
         timez i
          dont
          know
```

Alternatively, perhaps works such as "run tonight" can be regarded as raw material, the soupy verbal matrix from which moments of startling lyrical clarity emerge as we read through a bissett volume. By his own account, poetry is an abandonment of repressive rationality and ego distortions, an utterance of the "true" discoveries of untrammelled perception. He produces great wordfloods, evidently on the assumption that undirected consciousness will issue in something worthy of print. But it may also issue in the banal and the unintelligible, poems equally as bad as those "made up" by the excessively self-conscious poet. Voyagers through strange seas of thought and language risk shipwreck as they seek new worlds, and numerous of bissett's poems seem to me debris. Even so, the voyage is often worth the risk.

Though much of bissett's art is innovative, much is also fairly traditional in form, once one looks past superficial novelties of spelling and grammar. His versatility and vision overflow the forms of concrete and often issue in poetry that is both fluent and cogent. Notwithstanding his misgivings about doctrines and his diatribes against the tyranny of rational meaning, much of his work is full of meaning, and much is "message" poetry of a distinctly didactic orientation. He has produced many fine poems of a traditional sort: long meditations, brief lyrics, satiric narratives. These are more accessible than much of his experimental work, and it is probably no coincidence that one of his more conventional volumes has been praised as one of his best. In his review of *Pomes for Yoshi* (1972), Stephen Scobie confronts the question of the nebulous relation between spontaneity and order in bissett's poetic, and he makes a strong case for bissett's ability as a craftsman of poetry, in the traditional sense. As Scobie points out, "in some of his longer satirical poems — I'm thinking especially of 'Th Emergency Ward' and 'Killer Whale' — the pretence of the poem's being an unadulterated recital of facts *is* surely just a pretence. These poems practice a kind of reticence, an ironic understatement, a refusal to comment which is in the end far more effective than any actual comment could have been. . . ."[4] Scobie rightly singles out for admiration a genre in which bissett excels, the "realistic" personal anecdote which becomes an avenue of social criticism. bissett's narrative versatility extends also to visionary romance and fantasy in poems such as "let me tell yu a story of how they met" in *Polar Bear Hunt* (1972), but I wish to follow up Scobie's judgement of "Killer Whale," from *Lost Angel Mining Company* (1969), as a particularly fine example of the realistic narratives.

Like many of Al Purdy's poems, this is a personal anecdote that implies a sweeping view of the impersonal present, together with a sense of fundamental values. The poet recounts a hitch-hiking episode with his lady, martina, during which they look at some captive whales. Their bad day becomes an indictment of our culture's bad times. The prevalent causes of tyranny and constriction in our lives dominate the environment the poem describes: corporate and bureaucratic institutions like MacMillan-Blodell, like the legal system which has "busted" the speaker — presumably for a marijuana offence, like the official policy which precludes charity in government employees (an attitude echoed in the indifference of the attendants to the suffering whales). Similarly, details such as bus schedules, phone booths and plastic bags, suggest the technologizing of our lives which threatens on occasion to overturn our sense of freedom. The whales are a magnificent embodiment of the vitality and beauty which our civilization assaults, and they also represent a natural community of creatures which contrasts with the social isolation of the human figures in the poem. Contrary to the generally spirited character of bissett's writing, "Killer Whale" is stamped by an almost Arnoldian despondency about psychic exhaustion inflicted by the contingencies and shocks of modern life:

after th preliminary hearing, martina
and me and th hot sun, arguing
our way thru th raspberry bushes
onto a bus headin for Van, on th ferry
analyzing th hearing and th bust, how
th whole insane trip cuts at our life
giving us suspicions and knowledge
stead of innocence and th bus takes
off without us from th bloody B.C.
government ferry — I can't walk too good
with a hole in my ankle and all why
we didn't stay with our friends back
at th farm — destined for more places
changes to go thru can feel th pull
of that heavy in our hearts and in th air

At least bissett and martina muddle through the disorder and anguish here, and reach their immediate goal, Vancouver, for what it's worth. bissett's skill at relating idiom, circumstantial detail, and an implicit vision of our world, is obvious in works such as "Killer Whale."

These works can also demonstrate that poetry need not be formally radical to undertake inquiries or discoveries. In *Pomes for Yoshi* (1972), we observe the speaker assessing and reassessing his thoughts and behavior, measuring his feelings against his principles — doing, in short, what good poets have always done in exploring the paradoxes of sexual love. This book is so clearly the issue of an articulate consciousness seeking a realization of its experience in language. And this is the point at which bissett's "trad" poems intersect with his experimental writing. A number of his more homogeneous volumes also illustrate the questing attitude — perhaps "groping" would be more precise — which informs his work. Volumes such as *Pomes for Yoshi, Th First Sufi Line* (1973), and *Yu Can Eat It at th Opening* (1974), are serially arranged: they are flowing congeries of ideas, perceptions, moods, which taken individually may well form satisfactory brief poems, but which also body forth a larger meditative context. *Living with th Vishyun* (1974) is similar, and different: a

157

collection of relatively spare and cryptic poems which often give the impression of memoranda from the poet to himself.

I have used the term "realistic" in speaking of those poems by bissett which reflect, and reflect upon, his experience in a world which we recognize as the familiar context of our daily lives. Such realism, especially in its comic and satirical perspectives, is one way bissett controls, amplifies, and makes compelling the visionary intervals in his work. Here I would suggest that bissett has affinities with those writers over the past two centuries whose work is impelled by a dialectic of irony and lyricism. Writers such as Blake, Carlyle, Melville and — closer to bissett's own time and space — Leonard Cohen, have sustained the most profound lyrical visions through an equally powerful sense of the comic. Their work testifies to a peculiar feature of modern history: that glimpses of sublimity can be achieved only within a frame of irony. With these writers bissett shares, variously: a wish to exhort and inspire; an undertaking to express and interpret a whole epoch and culture; a distrust of reductive interpretation and a subversion of linear conventions; a taste for both epigrammatic brilliance and verbal luxuriance; and certainly not least, a delight in *playing* with language, an obsession with wordcoining, puns, jests, and a relish for sound and rhythm. Some of these qualities, especially the lyrical genius which complements bissett's realism, are concentrated in a poem from *Awake in th Red Desert* (1968):

song composd just after th alarm clock
before going to social assistance

who was that in th red boat
riding down sugar lane

who was that in th red boat
riding down sugar lane

who did yu see in th red boat
riding down sugar lane

who cud yu hear in th red boat
never to hear again

who cud yu hear in th red boat
never to hear again

Commentaries on poems like this one inevitably risk the
appearance of millstones appended to ponies. I think,
nevertheless, that "song" illustrates precisely my point
about an ecstatic vision within an ironic frame. Some of the
most crucial Romantic perspectives are here: the discovery of primordial glories in dreams and childlike
imagination, and the loss of this magic upon wakening to
the world of experience. The rhythms are those of
children's chanting games or ritual incantation, qualities
which permeate many of the visionary poems in *Th High
Green Hill* (1972). But before looking further at the world
conjured up in the course of bissett's song, I want to
consider the world referred to in its title.

  bissett's criticism of social and political structures is as
radical as his subversion of literary conventions. Indeed,
he believes they are fundamentally related. As a social
critic he is representative of the counter-culture, that con-
spicuous if nebulous rebellion which blossomed in the
sixties against traditional North American mores and
institutions. bissett locates the center of social corruption
in the United States and identifies "Amerika" as the source
and symbol of heartless, devouring modernism, the
Moloch against which Ginsberg raised his howl in the
fifties. bissett's treatments of this theme range from
relatively ironic, dramatic works like "Killer Whale" to jere-
miads like "LOVE OF LIFE, the 49th PARALLELL," in
Nobody Owns th Earth (1971), in which sides are quickly
chosen up and a torrent of accusation is loosed against the
invasion by "plastik" American culture which (bissett
believes) is destroying some kind of tutelary spiritual
presence in the Canadian landscape. The outrage that

159

vibrates through the long lines of this poem seems to quicken its tempo as the indictment surges forward. The repulsive imagery of American "power / sadism" is brilliantly chosen. Though the rhetorical violence of the poem makes me suspect the strict accuracy of the historical view proposed, it is clearly intended, like "Howl," as a rallying cry for rebels, not as a scholarly investigation.

The political affinities of the counter-culture are with socialism, in the priority it gives to collective values and anarchism, in its loathing of centralized government and bureaucracies. Hence its members are frequently interested in primitive societies, especially the Amerindian culture which they regard as both a victim of and a saving alternative to the infernal structures of modernity. A facet of the Canadian counter-culture, as we can see in "LOVE OF LIFE," is an espousal of nationalism as a way of resisting "American" values, especially individualism, in the interest of evolving communal societies. The pervasive problems of "identity" in modern life are met by a renunciation of ego, an abandonment of the contingencies of our individual identities in favor of a sense of tribal relationship. For the present, survivors of the counter-culture generally share a sense of underground solidarity as victims of persecution by the "straight" world of corporate interests, power politics, parental authority and police harassment. They shun careers in the service of the technological state, preferring the kind of lifestyle bissett aptly calls "gypsy."

One token of solidarity among the widely dispersed counter-culture nomads and their fellow travellers has been a lingo of stock phrases upon which bissett draws heavily in his work. It is a measure of bissett's talent that he can use this sublanguage so effectively, as Stephen Scobie pointed out in his review of *Pomes for Yoshi*: "Nothing but this consistency of tone could account for the way in which Bissett is able to use such terrible cliches of counter-culture jargon as "Far out', 'I can dig it', 'Heavy', and 'Got to get my shit together' with such complete honesty that the reader accepts them as being meaningful . . . ."[5] The same courage with which bissett resorts to

160

popular slang is evident in those numerous poems which risk a plunge into the maudlin. Simple feelings of love, delight, tenderness and wonder are the motives of many poems so direct and childlike that they are apt to baffle the hardearned worldliness of literary critics:

In th mushroom village
all th littul children
brightly smiling
in th mushroom village
all th littul children
brightly be
(from "Circles in th Sun," in *Lost Angel Mining Company*)

One of bissett's great gifts is his ability to make compelling poetry of feelings which may embarrass our tortuous sophistications or superficial notions of masculinity. As he says elsewhere, much to the point:

we have called
so much
sentimental
that we have
very little
left
perhaps nothing.
(from "The Caruso Poem," in *Awake in th Red Desert*)

Paramount among counter-culture attitudes is a revulsion from technological mentalities oblivious to simple human values. In *Th High Green Hill* bissett deplores our practice of "trying so hard to build we cant/ help but destroy." A distrust of systems, analysis and judgement may express a crucial insight into our contemporary malaise, but it may also provide an excuse for intellectual mediocrity, puerile behavior, or bad poems. Sophisticated spokesmen of the counter-culture frequently attack the idea of progress as one of the principal motives in the

161

development of our civilization. Against the technician's view of time as linear, with a past to be studied and a future to be engineered, the counter-culture values moments of ecstasy achieved through drugs, music, sex and mysticism. And against the modernist view of nature as raw material to be exploited, the counter-culture perceives intrinsic value in natural things. This attitude is reflected in a preference for spontaneous over calculated behaviour, a respect for ecological values, a recoil from urban living, a regard for the wilderness as a source of spiritual nourishment and a reverence for the human body. bissett's poetry teems with references to biological functions and rhythms: vision, breath, heartbeat, blood circulation, excretion, copulation. Many of his poems present grim interludes of city-dwelling and images of desolation row. In others, seeking a liberation from the oppressions of history, he celebrates a paradisal relation of man with the natural world. His commitment to these values is not, however, without certain paradoxes: the general denunciation of order, but the systematic precision of some of his designs; the devaluation of ego, but the production of an enormous *oeuvre* under his name. And in his recourse to stereo recording to disseminate his sound poetry, there is perhaps a trivial clue to an important principle: that technology rightly employed may after all be the best way for the general population toward that condition of freedom and pleasure sought by the counter-culture.

But the implications of bissett's poetics and politics are apt to divert our attention from the first things we notice about his books: the quirks of format and content, the visual whimsy, the ingenuous lyrical beauty, and the rhapsodic power. This last quality I consider the sign of his most important work, the visionary poetry in his longest volume, *Th High Green Hill*. Though it includes a few collages, wordgames and concrete experiments, this book is largely made up of brief visionary lyrics and long visionary meditations. I suggested earlier that bissett's sound poetry has a religious dimension. His performance on the LP which accompanies *Medicine My Mouth's on Fire* expresses the attitudes which inform traditional hymns, prayers and sermons. These attitudes are also implicit in *Th High Green Hill*, which offers a vision of spiritual redemption and fulfillment. Many passages delineate grimmer realities: the damage to nature and to people wrought by corporate exploitation and technological processing. The irony and rage which we observed in bissett's political poems provide the minor theme of the book. "America" appears again as the exemplar of all that is destructive in the exaltation of egotism as a personal and political philosophy. But the major theme is a transformation of vision and a recovery of those blessings of joy, beauty and mystery, of which modern culture deprives us:

   late 1971 distance, when thr is
no dawn, too many dumb side trips, i wanna go

   home, is home ths night, wher are th birds th flowrs
   th changing earth th real cold th hard togerhr work in
   all ths enslaving comfort

   The idea that the transformed vision involves a change in our relation to the natural world, indicates bissett's affinities with the great Romantic visionaries. Though the concern with vision exists throughout *Th High Green Hill*, the most explicit development of the theme occurs in a similar though much shorter volume, *Polar Bear Hunt* (1972). Here bissett insists that we need only cultivate "th eye uv th soul" to end the spiritual exile suffered through our habitual way of seeing the world. (We may recall Blake's distinction between imaginative and corporeal sight.) We suffer from our conviction that we see most clearly when we divorce ourselves "objectively" from the world around us. Objectivity is for bissett a life-denying stance, the hallmark of egotism and the rationale for destruction; he urges our *participation* as whole creatures in the glories of our world, whether through dreams, imagination, love or celebration. As expressed in one of the chants in *Th High Green Hill*: "yr heart is th eye uv th universe." He urges an opening up of our responses to the world we inhabit. Abandoning the ego, we become fit for

163

revelation and enter into ecstasies.

Many of the poems in *Th High Green Hill* evoke these ecstasies. Their language and structures reflect the awareness of plenitude, beauty, and mystery which is their main theme. If the style often becomes opaque, it seems less a reflection of vagueness in the experience than of the inadequacy of language to describe it. "Th breath" is perhaps the most splendid of bissett's visionary poems. The poet's sense of union with the world around him is conveyed through sharply realistic images of woodchopping, cooking, and a vivid evocation of a winter camp in a forest by the sea. We understand that the palpable measure of things is our own body and its rhythms, not the abstract criteria by which we generally mark the passing of time or the extent of space — these are merely "veils/ to pass thru," as bissett puts it elsewhere. Images of steaming breath, of smoke rising from a woodfire, and of mist rising from a river, affirm the spiritual identity of natural things. Perhaps the harmony of visionary experience and physical realities in bissett's poetry can best be illustrated by one of his brief lyrics, "snow cummin":

it takes just about
one tree fr a weeks
fire wood

our arms thru th branches

ther was a moose out
ther last three nights
calling

     nd one night last
week pack a wolves howling
ther cries cummin from back
a ways ovr th pond sum funny
clouds passin ovr the moon
a strange charge nd th blood
was up high thru th dreams

yu can see th frost in th air

th original plan

yu put on yr shirt in
th early morning nd its a
sheet uv ice ovr yr skin

yr blankets uv hair kiss th
blew tits rise in yr mouth
th white snow flyin all aroun
th warmth th trees green

fingr th sky

Notice the rich associations between the images of this extraordinary poem — the iconic unity of man and tree suggested in the lines on getting in the firewood; and the way the erotic images bend our attention back to the title, "snow cummin," which then becomes a metaphor for the onrushing seed that seals the union of man and woman in the greater unity of earth, sky and forest. And what is "th original plan"? Merely the poet's morning routine? Or perhaps the breathtakingly beautiful communion with the land, which our race has somehow forsaken?

The "return to nature" is such a popular cliche and a persistent theme in our literature that there can be no question of its psychic pressure in our lives. Throughout *Th High Green Hill* bissett recharges the most common images of nature with mystery and radiance: birds, flowers, hills, ice, snow, grass, animals, stars, sun, moon, earth, air, fire, water — all recover their primal power as kindred presences in our lives.[6] Two images especially seem to acquire a crucial symbolic meaning: waves, as a trope for breath, continuity, duration; and fire, as the spiritual incandescence in natural things. The long meditations — "WILD FLOWRS ABOVE TH TREE LINE," "th high green hill," "MEDICINE," "th mountain," "lettrs (for a passing comet," and "PRAYRS FOR TH ONE HABITATION" — variously develop bissett's visionary themes:

desire for the eclipse of the established order and the rise of an ecstatic community, the quest for a faith to endure and discover primitive ways, the prophesying of ancestral voices. Some of them share a common pattern: beyond the doubts and anger they express, they close with a rising crescendo of affirmation, a sense of homecoming to the land, to the present, to the blessings of the green world.

"PRAYRS FOR TH ONE HABITATION" begins by considering the treacheries and possibilities in words. Like so much of bissett's work, it merges comic realism with lyrical vision. The poet leaps out of bed, urged by a sense of imminent revelation and runs smack into the wall. The admission to the poem of this level of human experience makes us the more willing to take its higher vision seriously. And of course, "higher" is the wrong word to use. bissett envisions not a transcendence of "th one habitation," but a revelation of its beauty and fullness through our departure from personal obsessions and a tremendous intensification of our powers of apprehension. The poem implies a reverence for the elemental forms of life. "Animal" is no more a pejorative term for bissett than for the North American Indians with whom he shares a sense of affinity with other creatures, a respect for the powers of nature, and a desire to participate in rather than master the natural world. The meditation turns toward the question of evil — the destitution wrought by our social and political systems on the creative core of our beings (one thinks of R.D. Laing's similarly passionate indictment). We are:

mind creatures trying to influence nature
telling th tree its beautiful then cutting it down
  pouring concrete on its roots, more parking lots
    for anothr thousand years, more gasoline

    more amerikan controlled middul east crises
    for th oil rights, more parks and zoos, museums of
    th last exampuls of ths life forms, befor
      fossilized professors take ovr sayin class once

      ther was a planet.

The poem ends with a mighty song celebrating the earth and all of its natural forms as *home*, reminiscent of apocalyptic passages in Romantic and modern poetry from *The Prelude* to "Sunday Morning."

Though the motif of pilgrimage in some of bissett's meditations, and his emphasis on achieving bliss through a kind of self-renunciation, suggest parallels with the great world religions, his work reflects more closely the values of primitive religion. Theodore Roszak's last chapter in his study of the counter-culture is on the relevance of that powerful figure of primitive cultures, the shaman, whose vocation is his sensitivity to the sources of mystery and wonder in life:

> While the shaman may be one especially elected and empowered, his role is to introduce his people to the sacramental presences that have found him out and transformed him into their agent. Similarly, the artist lays his work before the community in the hope that through it, as through a window, the reality he has fathomed will be witnessed by all who give attention. For the shaman, ritual performs the same function. By participating in the ritual, the community comes to know what the shaman has discovered. Ritual is the shaman's way of broadcasting his vision; it is his instructive offering. If the artist's work is successful, if the shaman's ritual is effective, the community's sense of reality will become expansive; something of the dark powers will penetrate its experience.[7]

This comparison of shaman and artist bears upon the religious dimension of bissett's work; indeed, in performing his sound poetry, bissett often passes over completely from art to ritual. And the willingness with which he has suffered deprivation and persecution for the sake of living a life consistent with his vision, is not unlike the shaman's arduous discipline for the sake of cultivating his powers.

Many of bissett's drawings and paintings also reflect the primitive sympathies in his vision. Numerous designs in his volumes resemble the petroglyphs which continue to

```
                    ta rattul
                 rattul i wann
                ta rattul i wanta
            i wantaa rattul i wan
        i wantsarattul i wannta
    rattul i wanta a rattul ii
      want a rattul i wantaa
        rattul i wanta raaaa
          ttul i wanta raaaa
            tul i want aaaa
              rattul i waaa
                anta raaaa
                   tul i w
                   ant a
                   raa
                   tul
                   raa
                   tul
                   taa
                   raa
                   tul
                   iaw
                   ant
                   ara
                   tul
                   wan
                   taa
                   raa
                   tul
                   wan
                   taa
                   raa
                   tul
                   raa
                   tul
                   iwa
                   nta
                   raa
                   tul
                   wan
                   taa          168
                   wan
                   tsa
                   raa
                   tul
```

be discovered in the Canadian wilderness, remnants of the sacred arts of various Amerindian tribes. As though expressing the spiritual energy which (the Indians believed) pervades nature, bissett's favorite designs are peculiarly fluid, suggesting the shapes of flames, or sunbursts, or flowers, or wings, sometimes simultaneously. His drawings have a primordial quality: ample space, simple lines, a curious brilliance. Perhaps their most significant motif is the interpenetration of the human anatomy with elemental images of the world's body: waves, sun, mountains, hills, trees. The human or semi-human figures often suggest primitive people and their priests, or gods. Some of the latter, with fiery heads and great sweeping wings, are reminiscent of the rock paintings in Margaret Atwood's novel, *Surfacing*, which narrates a flight from civilization and a rediscovery of sacred powers in the Canadian forest.

A final point I'd like to make about bissett is beautifully illustrated in a concrete poem near the end of *Th High Green Hill*. This "rattle poem" is a delightful visual pun: there is no need for me to comment on the appropriateness of its shape and "sound." But I think it's important to ask, who uses rattles? And of course the answer is, two sorts of people: babies and shamans. "I wanta rattul" could be merely a peremptory demand for the toy, but it can also mean, for the baby, "I want to play," and for the shaman, "I want to perform a ritual." Nor are these last two meanings very distinct from one another. As Johan Huizinga has suggested, ritual and play are intrinsically related, and express impulses which may also issue in poetry — especially lyric poetry, which comes "closest to supreme wisdom but also to inanity."[8] Such an insight can illuminate the main features of bill bissett's art: its affinity to the primitive; its frequently enigmatic quality; its heavy use of repetition; its subversive intent; its exuberance, its capriciousness, its moments of astounding beauty and power. It may also give us some understanding of one of the most marvellous of his achievements: the demeanour of perfect seriousness and absolute delight, simultaneously. Perhaps this is one of the rich dimensions missing from our lives — at least, since we grew up.

169

[1] *From There to Here* (Erin, Ontario: Press Porcepic, 1974), p. 50.

[2] *An Anthology of Concrete Poetry*, edited by Emmett Wiliams (New York: Something Else Press, Inc., 1967), n.p.

[3] *Surrealism: Theatre Arts, Ideas* (New York: Harper and Row, 1972), p. 17. For an account of the relation of contemporary concrete poets to Dada, see Stephen Scobie, "I Dreamed I Saw Hugo Ball: bp Nichol, Dada and Sound Poetry," *Boundary 2*, III, No. 1 (Fall 1974), 213-225.

[4] "Bissett's Best," *Canadian Literature*, No. 60 (Spring 1974), 121.

[5] *Ibid.*, 122.

[6] Frank Davey makes a similar point about bissett's vocabulary in *From There to Here*, p. 51.

[7] *The Making of a Counter Culture* (Garden City, New York: Doubleday, 1969), p. 260.

[8] *Homo Ludens: A Study of the Play Element in Culture* (Boston: Beacon Press, 1955), p. 142.

Atwood's Gorgon Touch

Frank Davey

In the opening poem of Margaret Atwood's first book, *Double Persephone*, a "girl with the gorgon touch" walks through a formal garden searching for "a living wrist and arm."[1] But she finds only "a line of statues" with "marble flesh." This "gorgon" is apparently Medusa, whose glance turned men to stone. In the concluding poem of Atwood's recent collection of new work, *You Are Happy*, another male figure appears with similarly sculptural qualities:

> On the floor your body curves
> like that: the ancient pose, neck slackened, arms
> thrown above the head, vital
> throat and belly lying
> undefended . light slides over you, . . . (96)

But this statue comes to life, is willed by the voice of the poem out of the worlds of art and ritual and into that of flesh:

> this is not an altar, they are not
> acting or watching

You are intact, you turn
towards me, your eyes opening, the eyes
intricate and easily bruised. . . .

("Book of Ancestors," 96)

In the seven books of poems which lie between these
passages, this opposition between the static, the mythological, or the sculptural and the kinetic, the actual, or the
temporal has been a central concern. Atwood's consideration of this opposition has been simultaneously ethical and
aesthetic; all attitudes toward form in her work have been
subject to moral judgements. The sources of this antithesis lie in the earliest days of Anglo-American modernism. Its deepest roots are in T.E. Hulme's rejection of
nineteenth-century empathetic realism for "some geometrical shape which lifts him [man] out of the transience
of the organic" and in the searches of Proust for "the real
without being of the present moment" and of Pound for "a
fragment of time in its pure state." Throughout Margaret
Atwood's poetry such goals are presented as attractive,
attainable — in terms of both life and poetic form — but
ultimately unsatisfying. The formal garden can be created
and entered, but its marble flesh cannot be lifted from still
dance into dancing life. Roles for lovers can be created and
enacted in *Power Politics*, but the enactments cannot be
relieved of a stylization which Atwood characterizes as
both artistic and deadly. The lovers become lifeless
statues:

Your face is silver
and flat, scaled like a fish

The death you bring me
is curved, it is the shape
of doorknobs, moons,
glass paperweights

Inside it, snow and lethal
flakes of gold fall endlessly
over an ornamental scene
a man and woman, hands joined and running. (56)

In "Progressive Insanities of a Pioneer" (*AC*, 36-39) a farm can be created in formal images of fences and furrows, but it cannot be obliged to yield an ordered life. Here not only does art not bear life, but it loses even its own sterile order and predictability when shattered by "the unnamed whale" of temporality and process.

This kind of poem, which makes up the bulk of Atwood's work, is overtly and normatively concerned with aesthetics — the role of the artist, the nature of form, and the relationship of form to historical time. One can choose the aesthetics of space — style, sculpture, ritual, static beauty — or the aesthetic of time — flesh, earth, and process:

Love,   you must choose
Between two immortalities:
One of earth, lake, trees
Feathers of a nameless bird
The other of a world of glass,
Hard marble, carven word.

(*DP*, 13)

Many of Atwood's poems rest on this antithesis. "The animals in that country" — "ceremonial," "elegant," "heraldic," "fixed in their tapestry of manners" — are posed against the animals of "this country" that have "the faces of animals" and eyes that "flash once in car headlights / and are gone" (*AC*, 2-3). In "At the Tourist Center in Boston," a "white relief map" of Canada "with red dots for the cities" is poised against a reality of "slush, / machines and assorted garbage" (*AC*, 18-19). The imagery of alienation from process is even more overtly presented in "Totems" where the antithesis is between restored museum-display totempoles and an unrestored totempole fallen and neglected. The former are described as "static," "uprooted and transplanted," and as analogous to the tourists — "the other wodden people" — who pose nearby "for each other's cameras"; the latter is said to have "a / life in the progressing / of old wood back to / the earth, obliteration // that the clear-hewn / standing figures lacked." The images are again sculptural — "clear-hewn," "static," "pose" —

173

versus the temporal — "decay," "progressing." The poles have been taken out of time (uprooted both from the earth and from the culture which created them) and inserted into space — into a "park," into "cameras," and into "replicas and souvenirs" (*CG*, 59-60).

The camera, as above, is a frequent symbol in Atwood for the conversion of time into space. The poem "Camera" (*CG*, 45-46) describes a "camera-man" who in his search for an "organized instant" asks reality to "stop," to "hold still":

> you make me stop walking
> and compose me on the lawn;
>
> you insist
> that the clouds stop moving
> the wind stop swaying the church
> on its boggy foundations
> the sun hold still in the sky. (45)

His subject, however, insists in turn that the spatial correlative which the camera creates is itself a participant in temporality:

> Wherever you partly are
> now, look again
> at your souvenir,
> your glossy square of paper
> before it dissolves completely. (45)

Despite the time-fixing and light-fixing act of photography, historical time moves at nearly "the speed of light" to ravage both the photograph and the objects the camera-man hoped to save from time; ultimately the church is reduced to "a pile of muddy rubble / in the foreground" and the woman to a "small black speck / travelling towards the horizon / at almost the speed of light" (*CG*, 45-46). Two other poems that use photographs with disappearing subjects to argue the incompatibility of the art-object with temporality are "This Is a Photograph of Me" and "Girl and

174

Horse, 1928." In the first the "drowned" narrator claims to be "in the lake, in the center / of the picture, just under the surface" — presumably under the surfaces of both the lake and the photo. Her appearance in the photograph is not a spatial phenomenon; it takes place in time — "if you look long enough / eventually / you will be able to see me" (*CG*, 11). Temporality lurks, we may conclude, under the deceptively solid surfaces of appearance. In "Girl and Horse, 1928" the voice of the poem speaks from outside the photo to its girl-subject, insisting that her smile and her peaceful surroundings are illusory:

> Why do you smile? Can't you
> see the apple blossoms falling around
> you, snow, sun, snow, listen, the tree
> dies and is being burnt. . . .

Like the formal garden of *Double Persephone*, this illusion is an attractive one. In actuality, the "instant" of the photo ceases immediately:

> (on the other side
> of the picture, the instant
> is over, the shadow
> of the tree has moved.   You wave,
>
> then turn and ride
> out of sight through the vanished
> orchard, ...

But its illusion of permanence can bewitch the human mind, can become a "secret / place where we live, where we believe / nothing can change, grow older." The girl rides from the orchard "still smiling," in apparently happy ignorance of the effects of time (*PU*, 10).

As one reads through Margaret Atwood's body of poems, one finds her constructing a catalogue of evasions, evasions that are all extensions of this human need to "believe nothing can change." All represent an aesthetics of space and a denial of time. One is classical mythology —

the formal gardens of Medusa in *Double Persephone* and of Circe in "Circe / Mud Poems" of *You Are Happy*. Another is popular mythology — the Superman figure of "They Eat Out" in *Power Politics*, the comic book heroes wearing "rubber suits" of "Comic Books vs. History" in *Procedures for Underground*, or the "starspangle cowboy" with "porcelain grin" of "Backdrop Addresses Cowboy" in *The Animals in That Country*. Closely related is popular art — formulaic, "endless," and "stale":

> You take my hand and
> I'm suddenly in a bad movie,
> it goes on and on and
> why am I fascinated
>
> We waltz in slow motion
> through an air stale with aphorisms
> we meet behind endless potted palms
> you climb through the wrong windows.

(PP, 3)

Technology provides various ways of evading time: the camera, the blueprint ("The City Planners," *CG*, 27), or the museum ("The Circle Game," *CG*, 41; "A Night in the Royal Ontario Museum," *AC*, 20-21). A part of all of these is the philosophic evasion of humanism, the evasion of Atwood's pioneer who asserts man's timeless centrality in a processual nature palpably without centres. This poem, "Progressive Insanities of a Pioneer," contains Atwood's most vigorous portraits of the humanist:

> He stood, a point
> on a sheet of green paper
> proclaiming himself the centre,
>
> with no walls, no borders
> anywhere; the sky no height
> above him, totally un-
> enclosed
> and shouted:

176

Let me out!

(AC, 36)

The pioneer's sensibilities are spatially oriented throughout the poem; he is appalled by the absence of walls and borders: he constructs a house, fences, furrows, in stubborn resistance to the fact that "unstructured space is a deluge." He attempts to name the objects in his environment — to use language's abstracting power to lift them out of time and into the spatial categories of generic reasoning. However,

> Things
> refused to name themselves; refused
> to let him name them.   (39)

Ultimately, time triumphs over space. The "unnamed whale" of process, Atwood tells us, bursts through his fences, his fields, his clearings, and his subject-object categorizing mind. By implication, the aesthetics of space and of the humanist ordering of space are also discredited. The land here is metaphorically the raw material of any art — of love, husbandry, architecture, poetry; the farmer is the artist-lover of *Double Persephone* with his choice between "earth, lake, trees" and "a world of glass, hard marble, carven wood."

The Journals of Susanna Moodie narrates a similar struggle between time and space. This theme is signalled in the opening poem in which Mrs. Moodie laments that "the moving water will not show me / my reflection." She sees her adversaries as the sun ("The Planters," 16-17), change ("The Wereman," 19), unpredictability ("First Neighbours," 14-15), and "fire" — both literal fire and the "fire" of seasonal process" ("The Two Fires," 22-23). She attempts to defend herself through time-denying form:

> . . . concentrate on
> form, geometry, the human
> architecture of the house, square
> closed doors, proved roofbeams,
> the logic of windows.   (22)

But the "white chaos" (23) of her environment continually insists itself upon her as the only reality. Whiteness and light, frequent images in Atwood for camera-defying cosmic energy, surround and absorb her. A photograph taken in her old age documents her temporality rather than arresting it:

I orbit
the apple trees
white white spinning
stars around me

I am being
eaten away by light.
("Daguerreotype Taken in Old Age," 48)

Susanna Moodie's death removes her from all possibility of spatial illusion — from walls, manners, categorizations, and cliches "set up . . . at intervals" (55); it confronts her with raw process — here, as elsewhere in Atwood, metaphorically termed "underground." "Underground" for Mrs. Moodie is a "blizzard," a "whirlwind," a "holy fire" ("Resurrection," 58-59). It moves her in the last lines of the book to declare war on spatial structures and location:

I am the old woman
sitting across from you on the bus
....
out of her eyes come secret
hatpins, destroying
the walls, the ceiling

Turn, look down:
there is no city;
this is the center of a forest

your place is empty.
("A Bus Along St Clair: December," 61)

Such imagery of "underground" is one of Atwood's most important devices throughout her poetry for asserting the dominance of time over space. Time and process are subversive; they lurk under the surfaces of lakes, of photographs, under the ostensibly solid veneers of field and street. Process is liquid; substantiality — the basis of sculptural form — is an illusion man invents with his camera-eyes. Mrs. Moodie calls Canada a "land I floated on / but could not touch to claim" (30). The pioneer declares,

> The land is solid
> and stamped,
>
> watching his foot sink
> down through stone
> up to the knee.
>
> (*AC*, 38)

Appearances are thus duplicitous: the appearance of stasis conceals process; the appearance of order conceals chaos; the appearance of solidity conceals liquidity; the appearance of predictability presages surprise. The double condition of "double" Persephone, desiring process but receiving stone, is reversed for many of Atwood's later protagonists. The doubleness of reality for them lies in the invisible underpinning of temporality in ostensibly spatial objects. This doubleness requires a "double voice," one with "manners" and one with "knowledge" ("The Double Voice," *JSM*, 42), and a possession of "procedures for underground." Time-transcending devices — mythology, art, imagination, stylization — must be recognized as either weapons or crutches used by the weak in the face of mutability.

Many Atwood poems imply, like "Girl and Horse, 1928," that the need to deny temporality is understandably human; many others present a persona who gives herself with zestful ironic self-awareness to games, poses, mythologies, and sculptural perceptions:

We sit at a clean table
eating thoughts from clean plates

and see, there is my heart
germfree, and transparent as glass

and there is my brain, pure
as cold water in the china
bowl of my skull.

("A Meal," *CG*, 33)

The persona of *Power Politics* has this kind of ironic
awareness of her addiction to the aesthetics of the "circle
game." Her lover is another of the men of stone Atwood's
"gorgon" personae seem inevitably to encounter:

You stay closed, your skin
is buttoned firmly around you,
your mouth is a tin decoration,
you are in the worst possible taste.

You are as fake as the marble trim
around the fireplace, . . . (44)

His determined attempts to transcend time sometimes
involve commercial mythology — "suspended above the
city / / in blue tights and a red cape / eyes flashing in
unison" — and at other times political mythology:

in a year there will be nothing left
of you but a megaphone

or you will descend through the roof
with the spurious authority of a
government official,
blue as a policeman, grey as a used angel. (30)

His beloved, however, enters wholeheartedly into his
spatial assumptions about the world:

Put down the target of me
you guard inside your binoculars,
in turn I will surrender

this aerial photograph
(your vulnerable
sections marked in red)
I have found so useful. (37)

Much of the charm of this book resides in the woman's
mocking use of the man's spatial aesthetics and in the
frankness of her entry into a mutually exploitative
relationship. He wishes to be a statue; she treats him like
one. He acts insensitively, selfishly; she decided she can
be equally happy with a useful corpse as with a sensitive
lover:

I approach this love
like a biologist
pulling on my rubber
gloves & white labcoat
....

Please die I said
so I can write about it. (10)

Here again a doubleness asserts itself. Games are sterile
but fascinating; statues are cold but beautiful; illusory
order is false but addictive; the game of "love" is
exhilarating, although not in any sense "loving." Beneath
these various paradoxes lurks the central one of space
subverted by time. "Power politics" for the persona is a
children's game of pretense and fantasy. The verbal wit of
the book suggests the exhilaration of gamesmanship
rather than the pangs of conscience. The self-irony
suggests both the double vision of Susanna Moodie and a
duplicitous "procedure" for fantasizing away the processual underground.
   The evidence of Atwood's first two books indicates that
these considerations of the ethical dimensions of aesthetic

systems have some bearing on Atwood's own aesthetics as a literary artist. In *Double Persephone* a direct link is visible between the formal garden inhabited by her personae and the formalism of the writing. Atwood exercises her own "gorgon touch" here — substituting formal rhythms and language for the colloquial language of historical time and replacing temporal characters with pastoral and mythological ones.

> The shepherdess with giddy glance
> Makes the amorous shepherd dance.
> While sheep hurtle the stiles for love
> And clouds pile featherbeds above.
>
> ("Pastoral," *DP*, 5)

In *The Circle Game*, a book with the thematic intention of discrediting the "games" by which mankind converts time into space, the language is more casual; and the surfaces of event, image, and characterization appear realistic.

> Love is an awkward word
>
> Not what I mean and
> too much like magazine stories
> in stilted dentists'
> waiting rooms.
> How can anyone use it?
>
> I'd rather say
> I like your
> lean spine
> or your eyebrows
> or your shoes. (70)

However, the "underground" of the writing of *The Circle Game* is not the processual underground of the pioneer's farm — it is impersonal, mythological, and spatial. One notices this undercurrent in the first poem, "This Is a Photograph of Me." The protagonist speaks as a dispassionate observer of herself. Presumably she speaks from the temporal world beneath the surface of the photo, and her detachment is only from the spatial world of the photographic image. But the aesthetic effect of the writing communicates detachment from both worlds: the language is factual, unemotional; the verbs are mostly ones of static condition; the concerns are spatial — where this persona is and of what size:

> I am in the lake, in the center
> of the picture, just under the surface.
>
> It is difficult to say where
> precisely, or to say
> how large or small I am. (11)

At times in *The Circle Game*, the detachment from the self and from the human world in general is so complete that people are present only by synecdoche:

> The small carved
> animal is passed from
> hand to hand
> around the circle
> until the stone grows warm
> touching, the hands do not know
> the form of animal
> which was made or
> the true form of stone
> uncovered.
>
> ("Carved Animals," 62)

Here, through the synecdoche of "hands" and the passive voice of the opening verb, the sculptural reality of the carved animal is made dominant. The syntax of the poem, which alternates "hands" and terms for the "carved animal" ("stone," "animal") in the subject position, further dehumanizes the "hands" by making them appear parallel if not equivalent to the carved stone. The language also has a strong sculptural quality: the diction is factual, and the rhythm dispassionate. By creating linguistically unlikely junctures counter to the natural speech-pauses in the language, the line breaks enforce an unmodulated and noncolloquial tone. The temporal dimension of language as an emotional and personal response to experience is thus largely eliminated.

This tendency to embody a spatial aesthetic permeates all of Atwood's poetry. At the most elementary level, many of the central statements of her poems are assignations of relative spatial position: "I walk across the bridge . . . You saunter beside me, . . ." (*CG*, 12). "In the background there is a lake, / and beyond that, some low hills . . . / I am in the lake, . . . " (*CG*, 11). "There is my country under glass, . . . and beside it 10 blownup snapshots . . ." (*AC*, 18). "When we were in it . . . now / we are out of it . . ." (*PU*, 18). Adverbial phrases of location play key roles in many of the poems: "kneeling on rock . . . above me . . . under my shadow" (*PU*, 8-9); "in this garden . . . outside the string borders . . . in the evening forest . . . in the bay . . . in another land" (*PU*, 16-17); "Upon the wall . . . around it . . . on the upper lip . . . on the skin" (*PU*, 46). Some poems combine such phrases with statements of spatial location to become entirely about relative spatial placement:

Beside this lake
. . . .
my sister in bathing suit continues
her short desolate parade
to the end of the dock;

against the boards
her feet make sad statements
. . . .
(I sit in a deckchair
. . . .
She moves the raft out
. . . .
        . . . The sun encloses
rocks, trees, her feet in the water, the circling
bays and hills. . . .

(Under my hand the paper
closes over these
marks . . .

The words ripple . . .
. . . towards the shore.).
("Younger Sister, Going Swimming," *PU*, 66-67)

Somewhat more revealing is the repeated concern of
many of the poems with making statements of condition.
The underlying implication of such statements is the
existence of static qualities — identity, colour, shape:
"This is before electricity . . . The porch is wooden, / the
house is wooden and grey . . . (*PU*, 7); "She is / a raw voice
. . . She is everywhere, intrusive as the smells . . . She is a
bulk, a knot / swollen in space . . . a raucus fact . . . immu-
table" (*AC*, 14-15). This concern with establishing the
essence of things is further indicated by the large number
of copula verbs in Atwood, especially in opening lines:
"Here there are no armies" (*PP*, 38); "You are / the lines I
draw around you" (*AC*, 60); "The streets are new" (*JSM*,
50); "Marriage is not / a house" (*PU*, 60); "There are two
of them" (*CG*, 68); "There are similarities" (*CG*, 57). In
Procedures for Underground and the later collections,
most of the verbs are in the simple present tense and
appear to indicate temporally uncircumscribed action.

The sun shines down

on two cars which have collided
at a turn-off, and rest
quietly on their sides

and on some cows which have come over,
nudge each other aside
at the fence, and stare.
("The End of the World," *PU*, 32)

The static effect is amplified here and elsewhere by the
selection of verbs denoting condition or minimal action —
"shines," "rest," "stare," "refuse," "permit," "become":

You refuse to own
yourself, you permit
others to do it for you:

you become slowly more public.

(*PP*, 30)

The temporal indeterminacy of such verbs can contribute
to the creation of mythological or surrealistic effects:

I keep my parents in a garden
among lumpy trees, green sponges
on popsicle sticks. I give them a lopsided
sun which drops its heat
in spokes the colour of yellow crayon.

They have thick elephant legs,
. . . .

("Eden is a Zoo," *PU*, 6)

On other occasions this indeterminacy suggests habitual
on-going action and psychological estrangement from
historical time:

I walk the cell, open the windows,
shut the window, the little
motors click
and whir, I turn on all
taps and switches

I take pills, I drink water, I kneel.

(*PP*, 19)

The result of such techniques is the removal of time as
an operative dimension from much of the poetry. The
speaker appears to be a spectator to her own life, standing
outside both this life and its temporal context. The
principle of cause and effect tends to disappear under
such circumstances; events become juxtaposed in space
rather than processually related. Such a condition prevails

in "Progressive Insanities of a Pioneer" where the natural "oceanic" action of the land is in no sense caused or precipitated by the pioneer who has juxtaposed himself to it. It prevails in "After the Flood, We" in which two lovers are introduced syntactically as parallel subjects — "I walk across the bridge . . . you saunter beside me" — inhabiting parallel but self-contained experiences:

I walk across the bridge
towards the safety of high ground

I walk across the bridge
towards the safety of high ground
....

gathering the sunken
bones of the drowned mothers
....

   you saunter beside me, talking
of the beauty of the morning,
not even knowing
there's been a flood.

(*CG*, 12)

The syntactic parallelism is both ironic, in implying the existence of a relationship that is etiologically nonexistent, and real, in specifying juxtaposition in space as the only operative link between its terms. A similar lack of cause and effect prevails between the lovers of *Power Politics* whose relationship, despite their physical interaction, also appears to be one of spatial juxtaposition rather than of mutual causation:

You are the sun
in reverse, all energy
flows into you and is
abolished, you refuse
houses, . . .

> I lie mutilated beside
> you; beneath us there are
> sirens, fires, ...

Here "you" and "I" are assigned parallel syntactic positions by the parallel syntax of "You are the sun" and "I lie . . . beside you." The spatial quality of the relationship is underlined by "beside" and "beneath"; the latter preposition joins the lovers to a list ("sirens," "fires") of spatially related objects. This use of parallel syntax to indicate parallel but noninterlocking relationship is one of the principal technical resources of *Power Politics*.

> You say: my other wives
> are in there, they are all
> beautiful and happy, . . .
>
> I say: it is only
> a cupboard, my collection
> of envelopes, . . .
>
> In your pockets the thin women
> hang on their hooks . . .
>
> Around my neck I wear
> the head of the beloved, ... (50)

In this instance the distinctness of the lovers is emphasized by the ironic contrast between the parallel syntax and nonparallel content. The woman's dialogue is a non sequitur to the man's; the items "around my neck" are similarly irrelevant to the items "in your pockets." No temporal or causal relationship exists within either pair of items. The links are spatial: the juxtaposed lovers, their syntactically juxtaposed pronouns, their syntactically juxtaposed "pockets" and "neck," and the general juxtaposition created by the stanza arrangement. The over-all effect is one of collage — collaged lovers, objects, and stanzas.

Atwood's most recent work in *You Are Happy* shows

little alteration in this manner of writing. A great number of poems are concerned with the making of statements of condition, in which verbs of action become indicators of states of being detached from temporal context.

> It is spring, my decision, the earth
> ferments like rising bread
> or refuse, we are burning
> last years weeds, the smoke
> flares from the road, the clumped stalks
> glow like sluggish phoenixes . . .
>
> ("Spring Poem," 22)

When a first-person pronoun becomes a subject of these verbs, a self-detachment occurs in which the speaker seems to stand outside the atemporal frame in which the self exists and to view this self as an object outside of process.

> History
> is over, we take place
> in a season, an undivided
> space, no necessities
>
> hold us closed, distort
> us.   I lean behind you, mouth touching
> your spine, ...
>
> ("Book of Ancestors," 95)

The very structure of many of the poems is spatial. Both sections and many stanzas in the multi-section poems ("Chaos Poem," "Tricks with Mirrors," "Four Auguries," "Head against White") appear to be in arbitrary sequence; no temporal logic would be offended by their rearrangement. Concluding lines gain their effect by the surprise of spatial juxtaposition rather than by temporal logic:

> . . . overhead the weak voices
>
> flutter words we never said,

our unborn children.

("Useless," 10)

imprint of you
glowing against me,
burnt-out match in a dark room.

("Memory," 11)

. . . I could wear them
around my neck and pray to them

like the relics of a saint,
if you had been a saint.

("Repent," 18)

This structural technique resembles both that of modernist collage and that of the transcendence-seeking poetry of the early Imagist movement. The link between the juxtaposed elements is conceptual rather than temporal; their juxtaposition introduces juxtaposed contexts which propose an heuristic rather than a causal relation.

. . . he slopes down,
....
. . . roped muscles leaping, mouth open
as though snoring, the photography
isn't good either.

("Newsreel: Man and Firing Squad," 8)

Atwood's use of personae in this book seems entirely designed to objectify conditions of being, to create a verbal sculpture of an abstract proposition. Such are the ten "Songs of the Transformed." The "singers" all speak from outside themselves and regard their actions as repetitious, if not eternal.

I crackle through your pastures,
I make no profit / like the sun
I burn and burn, this tongue
Licks through your body also.

("Song of the Fox," 40)

All have been, in fact, removed or "transformed" from time by human acts of mythology and stereotype. The Circe persona in the long poem "Circe/Mud Poems" appears designed to stand in place of Atwood's own life on an Ontario farm and to "transform" this life (much as the lives of the speakers in "Songs of the Transformed" have been transformed) out of its temporal context. The actual lovers become the mythological Circe and Odysseus; their farm becomes Circe's timeless island; their actual histories in time become the archetypal "story" of immortal woman and mortal man. Circe here is another Medusa-Susanna Moodie figure who dislikes the timeless world in which she has lived. Her island seems to her a place of "ennuie." Mythological men have become tiresome:

> Men with the heads of eagles
> no longer interest me
> or pig men, or those who fly
> with the aid of wax and feathers
>
> or those who take off their clothes
> to reveal other clothes
> or those with skins of blue leather.

She seeks relief both from the unreality of such men and from the atemporality of her island:

> I search instead for the others,
> the ones left over,
> the ones who have escaped from these
> mythologies with barely their lives;
> they have real faces and hands. . . . (47)

Odysseus, on the other hand, despite his knowledge that it would be death to submit to transformation out of time, is still tempted by the timeless qualities Circe possesses. He becomes passive and quiescent.

> The trees bend in the wind, you eat, you rest,
> you think of nothing,

your mind, you say,
is like your hands, vacant. (50)

He relaxes into the deathly unrealities of mythological story.

Don't you get tired of killing
those whose deaths have been predicted
and are therefore dead already?

Don't you get tired of wanting
to live forever? (51)

At times he seems to wish that Circe were not becoming alive, but would continue as a statue, a "woman constructed out of mud," one who "began at the neck and ended at the knees and elbows." Unlike a woman alive in historical time, such a statue would be "simple": "Is this what you would like me to be, this mud woman? Is this what I would like to be? It would be so simple" (61).

On the thematic level, Circe succeeds in escaping into time. Odysseus' fear of transformation releases the talismatic fist from her neck (57), and she becomes aware of two possible "islands," one repetitive and timeless —

. . . the arrivals,
the bodies, words, it goes and goes,
I could recite it backwards (69)

— and the other in history, embodying events that have "never happened":

The second I know nothing about
because it has never happened;

this land is not finished,
this body is not reversible. (69)

At the conclusion of this section, she and Odysseus appear to walk on this second "island." Technically, however, the poem throughout is detached, sculptural, and spatial. Circe's consciousness is deliberate, self-detached, depersonalizing, and objectifying.

We two eat
and grow fat, you aren't content
with that, you want more,
you want me to tell you
the future. That's my job,
one of them, ... (66)

Even at the end of the poem, where one is to assume she has returned to history, she speaks with a self-detachment that places her consciousness outside the temporal frame in which her body exists and which presents this body as principally an object in a spatial design:

We lick the melted snow
from each other's mouths,
we see birds, four of them, they are gone, and

a stream, not frozen yet, in the mud
beside it the track of a deer. (70)

The theme of escape from space into time recurs in Atwood's work as frequently as events circle back on themselves in Circe's mythological home. From the Medusa of *Double Persephone* who yearns for a man who will resist her transforming gaze to the woman of the final poem of *You Are Happy* who sees her lover awaken from a sculptural pose, Atwood concerns herself with the tyranny of atemporal modes — mythology, stylization, ritual, cultural stereotype, commercial image, social manners — and with the contrasting richness of kinetic reality. Yet for Atwood art itself seems inevitably to possess the "gorgon" touch and to work to transform life into death, flesh into stone. Almost all of her major personae are the artist-as-transformer: Medusa the statue-maker; the Power Politician who transforms her lover into a comic-book hero; Susanna Moodie who can remake her husband into her "idea of him" (*JSM*, 19); Circe who can make men into animals or "create, manufacture" hierarchic lovers (*YAH*, 47). The struggle of these figures to abandon art and enter historical time is enlarged by the extra-temporal aesthetic implicit in Atwood's use of language and form into Atwood's personal struggle. In its own doubleness this struggle is impossible to resolve without her abandoning the practice of writing; it is therefore repeated in differing dramatic contexts from book to book. In each book, the language she employs communicates to the reader the presence of a consciousness divorced from the very temporal universe it argues he should enter. The reader thus experiences vicariously the dissociations from time and the detachment from being which the Circle Game or the game of Power Politics creates. The power of the poems is amplified by the implicit information in their language and form that the consciousness behind them suffers victimhood from the forces that the poems decry. Like Circe and Medusa, this consciousness has pathological power which it does not want, has insight into process and foreknowledge of event which only its alienation from process allows. Like a mirror, it creates art at the expense of its own participation in reality:

Don't assume it is passive
or easy, this clarity

with which I give you yourself.
Consider what restraint it

takes: breath withheld, no anger
or joy disturbing the surface

of the ice.
You are suspended in me

beautiful and frozen, I
preserve you, in me you are safe.

It is not a trick either,
it is a craft:

mirrors are crafty.

("Tricks with Mirrors," *YAH*, 26)

Throughout Atwood's work the operative irony is that a voice, excluded from time but wanting in, owes its very ability to speak to the static forms made possible by its exclusion. Art, speech, and writing are "crafty"; they separate one from process and from one's kinetic self. Her personae, as above, and elsewhere in "The Circle Game," *Power Politics*, and "Circe/Mud Poems," taunt their lovers with this knowledge. If these men wish to make use of the transforming power of the lady-artist, they must forego the temporal woman they may also desire. Atwood's poems circle back on themselves, recreating one central drama of artist-woman engaged in an unsuccessful struggle to escape art for mortality. Essential to this drama is the implicit impossibility of resolution — an impossibility embodied in "the gorgon touch" with which Atwood's language, form, structure, and characterization are directed. Order here may conceal chaos, but only an embracing of order enables a speaking of either.

Something in which to believe for once: The Poetry of John Newlove

Jan Bartley

In a search to find a personal faith in something or anything which is not delusive, the perseverance of Newlove at least equals his pessimism. No one can deny the dominant shade of blackness in his poetry; but it is too easy to dramatize it, thereby ignoring any positive tones and even the occasional moods of optimism. By not divorcing form from content, Newlove's work can be read as a mixture of positives and negatives — his reluctance to either sugar coat or romanticize his vision has become the basis of the negative voice for which he is often criticized.

As early as 1968, with the publication of "Samuel Hearne in Wintertime" and "The Pride", Newlove rejects ideas of romanticism, tempting though they are, in favour of an unflinching look at reality. In the first poem, the image of the explorer, Samuel Hearne, striding gallantly "through the land for a book", becomes not only romantic but absurd because the knowledge of the country is external and cannot be mapped. What Newlove wants the reader to see and remember is "SAM", ordinary man, travelling with the Indians through a strange land and finally confronted with despair, terror, and death in the abrupt image of a speared Eskimo girl. Throughout the poem, Newlove bombards his audience with repugnant images; he describes the land not in a series of 'poetic' images suggestive of wild beauty, but in matter-of-fact and even dull terms. In the final stanza, in the final simile, the explorer and the poet are united in emotion and in the knowledge of death which must be confronted in order to attain any understanding of a harsh and cold environment.

In "The Pride", Newlove follows a similar pattern of reaching back from a rootless present to a past rich in legend and tradition. In a frenzied search for personal identity, he imposes upon a "desolate country" the mythic element of the Indian gods and legends. His language shifts from the factual accounts of a chronicler to a rhythmic series of images describing the Indian gods — gods at once exquisite and terrifying. In parts three and four of "The Pride", Newlove becomes (in a very non-typical stance) "bewildered/ son of all men" searching for an image to worship and a meaning which will bring completeness. The country of his present is tamed with orchards and fading hills but the way back to roots and "a half understood massiveness" is revealed in this chant of hope:

but the plains are bare,
not barren, easy
for me to love their people,
for me to love their people
without selection.

In section five, Newlove concentrates on the life style of the prairie people, on their relentless pursuit of the great herds and their acquaintance with "the luxuries of war and death". After the first eighteen lines of varying length which are written in a colloquial language, the poet switches to a tighter form and a more poetic rhythm to emphasize Indian knowledge and pride. The knowledge based on struggles of life and death is powerful; the pride stressed by quick movement and line endings becomes a statement of assurance which is almost hysterical:

relieved from the steam of knowledge,
consoled by the stream of blood
and steam rising from the fresh hides
and tired horses, wheeling in their pride
on the sweating horses, their pride.

The closing sections of the poem replace the loneliness of the middle verses with the significant use of the pronoun "we". Newlove joins with his audience; the prairie people become his ancestors; and their pride becomes rooted words, "the grand poem / of our land, of the earth itself." Thus, "in a line of running verse", it becomes our pride also. The tone of these sections ranges from awe to triumph and there are many phrases which suggest the magnitude of "the knowledge of our origins". No doubt the poet is ardent in his attempt to convince the reader (or to be convinced himself) of the synthesizing nature of his inheritance. He realizes that it must "shock our attentions", flood upon us like a "sunlight brilliant image" and leave us in amazement. Yet it is evident in the closing stanza that Newlove wants to believe in history regardless of the difficulty. The credibility of his thesis is weak, even naive when examined carefully; but the lure of rhythm and repetitive sound and the undercurrent of urgent identification make his position tempting:

and they
become our true forbears, molded
by the same wind or rain
and in this land we
are their people, come
back to life again.

The intention of "The Pride" is ambitious; and as a formula for national identity it is unsuccessful. But much of the poetry is remarkable and in view of Newlove's later work the poem stands as an interesting experiment. Here he is almost a prophet; here he finds positive solutions. If the weakness of his conclusions disturbs the reader no doubt they also disturbed the poet for nowhere else in his work is there such hope or positive statement again. However, the search motif is strongly established and it is not the role of explorer which changes but rather the nature of his discoveries.

Most of the remaining poems in *Black Night Window* focus on an internal search which is intensely personal and frustrating. It is difficult and perhaps dangerous to give a label to the final goal which Newlove pursues. Ultimate knowledge and 'Truth' have become workhorses of poetic definition that would make any poet suspicious, especially one as concerned with equivocation as Newlove. However, the search in *Black Night Window* is one that aims towards nakedness, towards a picture of man and reality that is stripped of clichéd roles and pretence. Whatever knowledge the poet gains in his examination and rejection of false fronts is often defined in terms of despair and death. The dominant tone of the book is established by the title poem:

Black night window-
rain running down
the fogged glass,

a blanched leaf
hanging outside
on a dead twig,

the moon dead,
the wind dying
in the trees,

in this valley,
in this recession,

The atmosphere here is dismal, even mournful. However, despite the emphasis on depression, it is possible to discover the mixture of positive and negative that is so often ignored in Newlove. What makes the poem so memorable is not its bleakness but its remarkable lyrical presentation. It is possible to emphasize the blackness of

Newlove's subject matter here, but by doing so one divorces the form and content of the poem and ignores its presentation. "Black Night Window" is not a morbid poem so much as a finely crafted expression of a particular state of mind. The middle lines of each of the first three stanzas contain participles which are framed by definite images. These images originate from a field of immediate external vision but eventually define a mental mood. This rhythmic pattern combined with the repetition of "dead" and "dying" and the preposition "in" at the beginning of each of the last three lines creates a haunting musical quality and saves the poem from flat gloom. Tone, form, and mood are interfused and, though the voice of the poet is dejected and lonely, the ability to create is in itself a positive or at least hopeful assertion.

In *The Cave*, Newlove exposes the fallacies of man with renewed intensity. But he does not see himself as a hero or as a figure of any remarkable stature. He is always at the core of his poems, caught in the same trap as those he either condemns or pities. The black world is not something he can stand back from and assess with any sense of complete detachment since, being human and aware of his own past and limitations, he is unavoidably caught within its boundaries.

The initial poem, "The Engine and the Sea", is a devastating beginning. Here, the landscape shifts from the spaces of the prairie in *Black Night Window* to steamy swamps, marshes and mechanically controlled cities. Both the human and natural worlds, juxtaposed throughout the poem, are desolate and threatening. The former is marked by hypocrisy and futility; the latter, by the "music of ominous living" and uncountable animal eyes":

...............Frogs touch
insects with their long tongues, the cannibal fish and
the stabbing birds

wait.

The effective repetition of the word "wait" takes on a

fearful connotation: "In the cities men wait to be told"; "frogs wait, fish, angling birds"; "fish wait under the surface of a pinked pool"; "the land waits, black, dreaming". Finally, "wait" forms an entire line spaced apart from the rest of the poem. One senses some nameless catastrophe, some imminent explosion which will shatter man's presence. "Men lie dry in their beds" with a false security, apparently oblivious to their ultimate vulnerability. The concluding five lines emphasize the elusiveness of man's struggle:

Frogs shiver in the cold. The land waits, black,
                                   dreaming. Men
lie dry in their beds.
History, history!

Under the closed lids their eyes flick back and forth
                                   as they try
to follow the frightening shapes of their desires.

The words "History, history!" are a farewell chant, a repudiation of "The Pride" which Newlove discards as a human myth.

The majority of poems in *The Cave* are single voice ones in which the poet or a persona struggles with everyday problems of alienation, loneliness and self-development. Here, too, there is a stress on disappointment and inadequacy. Memory and elements of dream and fantasy are dangerous and often lead their creator into almost brutal realizations. Occasionally, the sense of failure and/or self-pity is buffered by the delightful wit and irony of a poem such as "Remembering Christopher Smart"; but, for the most part, Newlove despairs, almost to the point of personal indulgence. In a remarkable line from "The Fat Man" he states, "Even the worst of dreams / sometimes fails to come true."

However, even in the midst of masochism and a self-created atmosphere of psychological revulsion, Newlove continues to develop his craft. His precise use of language, stripped of any poetic posturing, conveys exactitudes, not mere impressions. Witness, for example, the disturbed man in "Revenge" grinning with morbid impulse; the female snake in "You Told Me"; or the pathetic and desperate "Funny Grey Man", the power of which rests on effective understatement and the subtle nuances of the word "funny". In the actual process of creation, the confrontation with words and rhythm, Newlove finds his greatest hope and his greatest frustration. Concerned as he constantly is with accuracy, he has an enormous mistrust of words. Language is inadequate since it can only describe things rather than the essence of things. Newlove's poetic vision penetrates to the very bone of experience yet even the most accurate vocabulary can only scrape at surfaces. In "These Are Yours" he writes "But still, / polished words . . . / Shiny remnants / of our future dreams" giving language a tempting but artificial quality. Since he is always shrugging off disguises, the noticeable lack of decorous language and the use of a sparse and contracted form is consistent with his personal attitudes. The number of metaphors in *The Cave* could easily be counted on one hand. The most explicit statement of poetic theory is incorporated in the image of "The Flower":

I am too tense,
decline to dance
verbally. The flower
is not in its colour,
but in the seed.

Newlove is a superb craftsman, one who always zeroes in on the exact word or sound sequence or tone to convey meaning, and yet he is suspicious of conscious patterning. He resists the use of a standard form and is adept at the variation of line length and typography. He often lists images letting them stand as visual fragments without logical connection or emotional evaluation. Excerpts from "These Are Yours" and "Portuguese Cove" demonstrate this technique:

The snow sings
to the swaying trees.

Children do
their Indian imitations
indoors.

Dry yellow tobacco
drops to the floor

and:

Look how high the moon is,
a different colour now,

then orange, lemon now.

The sky was green,
the ocean: darkest blue.

Both are black now.

The majority of poems in *The Cave* have a prose-like
quality due to the use of colloquialism. Newlove seems
most comfortable and shifts his moods readily within this
type of speech. In "El Pas", which begins "Motel alone's /
a lonely bed / for a married man", his tone conveys a
desperate alienation; but in "Days From A Week" the
language creates humour:

The how-will-your-mother-feel-
in-heaven-knowing-you're-in-hell
transcendental blues. Me
neutral. I never use
I in a poem again
after tomorrow, ma. And
that's a promise from your boy.

Finally, the poem which deals most significantly with
Newlove's attitude towards both the human condition and

the act of poetic creation is "The Last Event". In his attack on history, the poet examines death and war in a horrific vision; however, the emphasis is on "warring love", on a much more basic violence which infects a society where man is man's enemy. His suspicion of language is included as one of man's arrogances; but, significantly, he refuses to condemn poetry, leaving it undefined — as something magnificent and beyond human reach:

> poems . . .

> No thumb-worn medallions of approved worth, gold,
> no bronze
> or
> silver loving cups of worth burning like the prairie grass
> on fire
> bright day when blueberry, strawberry, raspberry,
> chokecherry . . .
> wild chokecherry grows on the tree to fill the crippled
> throats of
> boys longing to say . . .

The last two lines of the poem relate back to the "crippled throat" and the desire for speech. Newlove implies that a perfect moment of communication will occur in death:

> The earth dissolves at last between the mind and
> his dark throat
> in that last animal event.

The barrier between the mind and the "dark throat", between what is known and what can be articulated, is finally dissolved creating a wholeness beyond any threat of falsification. Here, the frustration of a poet and the possibility that man cannot be redeemed unless by death is certainly negative. But the willingness to accept the "last animal event" and to see in it a special freedom is an important consolation. For through transcendence the crippled throat is healed and the hope of actually touching the magic of poetry is possible. The perfection which

Newlove demands is elusive but positive in that it provides something beautiful and eternal for which to strive.

The last entry of the collection is the title poem. In "The Cave" Newlove presents a new vision of existence which is strange but, I think, finally optimistic. It is a difficult poem to understand and cannot be approached without re-examining standard landmarks and barriers of the universe. The cave opens onto a new galaxy which is freer and more magnificent than the old. In the early sections of the poem the earth is seen as a postcard, the sun as a two-carat diamond and the stars as one-carat diamonds. A young girl, seemingly mortal because she is growing older, wears the sun on her hand; there is a suggestion that not only flesh but the universe as well is susceptible to decay:

The diamond glows on her finger
like a worm. The stars, the stars
shine like one-carat diamonds. Beyond
Pluto and the darkest planets the stars shine.

The diamonds shine in wormy rings
on fingers, in coffins of unobstructed space.
The flesh circles the bone in strips
in the coffin as the ring circled flesh.

The most important word in "The Cave" and the only one which is not ambiguous is "beyond". 'Beyond' there are no ideas to trap you; beyond Pluto children surround the female; beyond the darkest planets, the stars shine. Finally:

. . . Beyond the planets,
beyond the dark coffin, beyond the ring of stars,
your bed is in the shining, tree-lit cave.

By expanding his vision Newlove transcends the external world and reaches a space of freedom and infinite possibility. The final position of the poem and the repetition of "beyond" does much to balance the negative intensity which permeates the collection.

In *Lies*, Newlove's most recent collection, there is an emphasis on trickery and an undercurrent of wry humour but the major characteristic is ambiguity. The clever title may suggest an element of frivolity but the content of *Lies* is both serious and urgent. Newlove perseveres in his role as explorer and exposer refusing to be placated by either human myth or imaginative evasion. The falsity includes personal delusion, historical misconception and romanticism, and social roles and hypocrisy. Civilization itself is fraudulent. There is no element of surprise left for man and therefore his experience is one of perpetual routine and dehumanzation. Cities which are described as "the concentration camps of the soul" in "Like a River" are temporary despite their surface impressiveness. In "It is a City" Newlove writes "o Shining creation, when will you die / among the fishbones and the plastic weeds, / and let me lie?" Throughout the book the sea is "waiting" and as in *The Cave* the word implies a silent surprise and a persistent animal life which will outlast man.

Newlove's themes depict an unheroic people isolated both in time and from their emotions. A poem such as "Like a River" demonstrates how far Newlove is removed from the thesis of "The Pride". In both poems he follows a similar pattern, fluctuating between images of the past and present; but here, the past is cheapened. There is no mystical union, no ancestry, only aimless ghosts "wanting rest / and ownership, something in which to believe for once."

The central poem in *Lies* is "Notes From And Among The Wars". It is an extensive work involving twenty sections of varying length and form each of which explore the fallacies and vulnerabilities of either the poet or the human condition. The central theme is the desire to dream versus the impossibility of sustaining dreams or transcending reality by means of dreams. As Bowering says, "the lies are seen to be shared among poets and other idealists, those bitter ones, the lies they remember are promises told the innocent." Newlove refuses to perpetuate the lies; he slashes away at all pretences (including his own) and focuses on the "simple everyday savagery of parent to

child / or child to parent brother to brother sister to sister".
The violence is both fundamental and apparently endless
as the last two stanzas suggest:

> The torture goes on forever as we in perpetual motion
> breed and destroy ourselves for any reason
> even intelligent ones
>
> All of which we have always known
> in despair and amusement at ourselves

The impact of the contradictory words "despair" and
"amusement" fully exposes the courageous insignificance
of man. They also do much to describe the fluctuating
moods of Newlove himself in his constant exploration of
society and his relation to the cosmos.

Throughout *Lies* Newlove despairs of language but
refuses to abandon it. In "Or Alternately" he describes his
life as "reading books, making notes, writing words, words
— words, for God's sake!"; and then asks flippantly, "Why
can't I draw?". As in *The Cave*, the emphasis of his poetry is
craftsmanship and lyricism. He displays a versatility of
form ranging from prose paragraphs in "Or Alternately" to
the column-like patterning of words in "Of Time". A similar
range is evident in his choice of vocabulary. His language
and imagery is often startling — not at all poetic in the
conventional sense. In "I Do Remember You" both his
fascination with and repulsion by the female figure is
related by the following image: "One night I pulled up your
sweater / and your breast shone out like a disease / I'd like
to have." In "Six Disasters" he again rejects expected
romantic terms for the following description: "Sometimes
your arm is soft as a turkey's dead raw leg / and your voice
sounds like mashed potatoes / in your lechery". The
association that Newlove makes is certainly surprising but
somehow after reading it, it is difficult to imagine a
lecherous voice sounding any different.

Despite the frustration and despair inherent in Newlove's search, there are moments in his poetry when he
is able to find peace and hope through communication

and identification with his fellow man. As the youthful I in "The Hero Around Me", he thinks of the hero "as a man in combat only" and desires to join him for one instant in his "soldierly deeds". However, when the moment does come he discovers with delight a much more positive heroism:

> The day came, but not as war.
> Fields of grain around me were crystal,
> the sky polished, endless gold and blue,
> and in the still heat a meadowlark
> twisted its sculptured tune around me
> once, quickly, a deft feat of superior magic,
>
> and all time stopped, world without end,
> and I was as a tree is, loathing no one.

The words "polished", "sculptured", and "superior magic" suggest the craftmanship of art. Through poetry Newlove may hope to enjoy, if only for one suspended instant, something in which to believe for once.

Cohen's Life as a Slave

Eli Mandel

It is probably necessary to apologize for attempting a
serious discussion of Leonard Cohen's poetry, so quickly
do contemporary "media Creations", as one of our critics
insists on describing Cohen, become debased coinage. Of
course, his work does present actual problems. I remember once a high-minded Canadian poet taking me to task
because I chose to treat a cartoon poem of B.P. Nichol's
with high-minded critical seriousness. The subject, I was
told, was beneath me. And, another Canadian writer once
muttered to me darkly after seeing a performance of
Michael Ondaatje's *Collected Works of Billy the Kid*, "All
that beautiful language wasted on a character who is so
unsavoury." Certainly serious criticism of a writer like
Cohen suffers from the difficulty that he refuses to take his
work seriously: the victory of style over vision apparently
undercuts any attempt to elucidate his subject or to
examine his themes. But the effort, it seems to me, is
worthwhile not simply because, in his development as a
writer, he represents contemporary sensibility, but because his treatment of what, for want of a better term,
could be said to be the writer's problem, the difficulty of
being a writer, remains one of the most scrupulous and
uncompromising we possess. To speak of Cohen in these
terms, as a representative and uncompromised writer, I

realize will sound peculiar, the more so if one looks at a collection of poems like *The Energy of Slaves*, his latest book, apparently as shoddy a piece of work as one could find anywhere today.

Of course, it is precisely this question of shoddiness that concerns me in this paper. Most contemporary writing presents itself in ways that to a traditional critic of literature, or to one concerned with the central place of literature in a humanist tradition, will seem problematical. George Steiner, for one, devoted much of *Language and Silence* to the paradoxical situation that it is the best of the humanist tradition — humane knowledge, literacy, and civilizing intelligence — that has been put to the worst uses. And he remarks as well on the shoddiness of contemporary imagination, its attraction to dark and rubbish-strewn corners of human experience, its obsession with the irrational, the brutal, the inhumane. Consider, he says, the contemporary writer's concerns: the exalting of the criminal as saint in Genet's plays and novels; the brutish mockery in Wm. Burrough's mechanical manipulation of character; those human beings shoved into the ashcans of Beckett's drama; the saintly garbage heap of Ginsberg's America; the "mawkish sadism" — it is Steiner's term — of Tenessee Williams; or again to put it as he does, the "absurdly diminished and enervating view of human existence" implied by Salinger's "rococco virtuosity"[2]; we can add to the list: the elegant hollowness of John Barth's imitation of Borges; the shabby theatricality of Norman Mailer; the furtive pornography of Robert Lowell; poetry itself turned into featureless sound clusters, the ragged hallucinogenic mutterings and yowls of Michael McLure's tantras; or at best, the manic perceptions of Sylvia Plath in the terrible radiance that preceded her suicide; the syntactical contortions of John Berryman's *Dream Songs* rehearsing his own tortured leap to death. The list is random, but I hope typical. For it points to the dilemma of criticism confronted with intractable material, what Northrop Frye refers to as "reactionary and anti-social attitudes,"[3] "quite obviously silly, perverse, or wrong-headed,"[4] and what others, notably Charles Olson, Warren

Tallman, and Susan Sontag, have seen as a profoundly anti-humanistic impulse, a deliberate rejection of the myths, metaphors, and values of humanism.

There is a tendency now to speak of contemporary concerns with incompleteness, irresolution, fabrication as "post-modern", presumably with the implication that sometime about 1946 — no one will be precise about old-fashioned matters of chronology — the consciousness of Western man suffered a sea-change. That is to say, one definition of a very vexed development is to see it simply as anti-modern, an opposition to its immediate ancestors.[5] Recently Harold Bloom has created a minor sensation with his argument that great writing, writing of magnitude, consists of re-writing the past: sons turning themselves into fathers, Blake re-writing Milton, Eliot attempting to show that all previous English literature imitated him, criticism as misreading. But the contemporary impulse, to borrow a phrase from Robert Kroetsch, is rather to erase, un-write, un-invent the past, to write as if literature did not exist or had never existed, to create (if such a paradox is possible) an anti-art. And so while it is not my purpose to rehearse cultural history, I take it the cultural context to which Cohen's work responds is the one formulated as early as 1960 in Harry Levin's remarkable paper *What was Modern?* and recently taking on its Canadian shape in works as diverse as Frank Davey's *From There to Here*, Warren Tallman's "The Wonder-Merchants" and Kroetsch's own comments in *Boundary/2*. Kroetsch's words perhaps can serve as a summary: "He writes then, the Canadian poet . . . knowing that to fail is to fail; to succeed is to fail."[6] If this sounds like Victor/Victim formula made familiar by Atwood's *Survival*, it should surprise no one, though in detail, in the texture and drama of Cohen's poetry, it proves to be something different and I think more demanding.

The point of departure for this paper then is Leonard Cohen's *The Energy of Slaves*, and while the questions it raises are those by-now-familiar ones of "post-modern" theorizing, I think the extreme version given to them by Cohen's new poetry makes it worth going over the same territory once again. My argument is simply that *The Energy of Slaves* belongs in the context not only of Cohen's earlier work, from which it does not represent any radical departure, but also in the context of Cohen's reading of the contemporary writer's difficulties with art and language. I take *The Energy of Slaves* to be another variation of Cohen's continuing concern with the meaning of *transformation* or (in an older language) transcendence, its necessity for the writer, his inevitable failure. If we take the term "myth" in Sartre's sense — a naming ceremony repeating or re-enacting a personal drama — the mythic moment of Cohen's work appears to have something to do with bodily transformation, the metamorphosis of Ray Charles at the end of *Beautiful Losers*, for example, or the equally remarkable changes in the speaker of "The Cuckold's Song":

The fact is I'm turning to gold, turning to gold
It's a long process, they say,
it happens in stages.
This is to inform you that I've already turned to clay.[7]

The mode of address too is important. Cohen's lyrics of transformation vary from formally-structured songs addressed to a traditional lover/mistress, as in "Dead Song", to versions of the dramatic monologue, "The Cuckold Song" I suppose could serve as an example, through a variety of dramatic addresses in which the "you" spoken to becomes more or less explicitly the reader or audience. As in Margaret Atwood's "You are Happy", Cohen's later work, beginning with *Flowers for Hitler* and his songs, develops a murderously ambiguous seduction/repulsion pattern pointing, I think, to a troubled, difficult sense in his poetry of two conflicting demands, the demands of audience, the demands of art. The "you" of the poems, beckoning/beckoned, helps to work out a cultural dialectic of surprising complexity and consistency, stages in the process of transformation. Here, I trace out in a crudely schematic way some major patterns of Cohen's work that help to account for this dialectic and explain the meaning of transformation.

Three terms that can be used for convenience are "context", "persona", and "object", roughly corresponding to "field", "mode", and "tenor" in linguistics, or in less barbaric language, I suppose, "subject", "speaker", and "intention". The context for Cohen's first book, *Let Us Compare Mythologies*, is art; the persona, the artist; the object, vision or martyrdom. For his second book, *A Spice Box of Earth*, the context is love; the persona, the lover; the object, purification or priesthood; with *Flowers for Hitler*, the songs, and to an extent *Beautiful Losers*, the context becomes history; the persona, the junkie; the object expiation. This is an admittedly awkward way of pointing to a development in which Cohen's highly literary and academic early poems are succeeded by his love lyrics, among them eight or ten of the finest poems in the language, which in turn give way to ironic fantasies that presage the bitter attack on both audience and art in *The Energy of Slaves*. Abstracted from his ceremoniousness and rhetoric of ritual and lacking his imagery of hanged gods, mutilated lovers, angels, corpses, and demented saints, this scheme does less than justice to his work, but it throws a sharp light on a major design in his writing: the tension between art conceived of as a dream of perfection, a transforming power, and history experienced as a nightmare of monstrous proportions and imperfections. The subtle decadence of Cohen's earlier poems in which a dream of high art is flavoured with spicy hints of torture turns into the melodrama of the later poems in which a history of horror is flavoured with the spice of sexual fantasies. This is to say no more than that Cohen's work is a series of variations on a theme of sado-masochism, but at the same time to recognize the deepening nature of his vision in which the later poems pose — through image and manner — a disturbing question about the involvement of art and private fantasy in a public nightmare of dreadful dimension. Yet the answer apparently attemped by Cohen — a radical critique of humanism — turns into a parody of itself, grotesque manoeuvering in the labyrinths of personality, melodramatic posturing, the poet as Nazi or Junkie, main-liner instead of traditionalist. In brief, the question put by his poetry concerns the meaning of the poet's involvement in mass art and popular culture.

It is worth remembering, Cohen literally experienced the betrayals forced upon him by the mass audience he sought and found, particularly the betrayal involved in identifying a remote, timeless visionary world with the vulgar fantasies of popular culture. His characteristically mocking blend of stylized phrasing and pop imagery seems designed at once to exploit and make light of this indentification that clearly excites and disturbs him.

Like the earlier *Flowers for Hitler*, much of *Beautiful Losers* is devoted to exploring these secret links between art and mass culture. In fact, Cohen's manipulation of the new possibilities released by his paralleling of high with low culture accounts, I believe, in part for both the brilliance and popularity of *Beautiful Losers* which, on the face of it, ought to have been a staggering failure on the market because of its obscurity, complexity, and erudition. Yet its pyrotechnics of style and language, far from repelling an audience supposedly on the verge of literacy, brought new worshippers at the feet of still another guru of the sixties media. Still, to explain Cohen's success solely in sociological terms, it seems to me, is an exercise of monumental futility and vulgarity and (if it were not a contradiction in terms to say so) transient interest. More important than its popular success is the stylistic discovery Cohen exploited in his writing. I suspect that the extraordinary energy flowing through the book originates in Cohen's sudden understanding of the real driving power of his imagination. That dynamo proved, after all, not to be the literature and tradition hallowed in the English Department of McGill, and honoured in Cohen's revealing title of his first book *Let Us Compare Mythologies*, but the popular culture on which he had been raised and the personal fantasies which not only fed upon the fascist masters with a comic book mythos but sprang from his own obsessions. In 1962 at a conference of writers in Foster, Quebec, a gathering of a strange group called "English Writers of Quebec," Cohen, who had just won a CBC prize for a ms of poems entitled *Opium for Hitler*, an early version of the later *Flowers for Hitler*, announced his new literary programme. Henceforward, he told the startled group that included such imposing figures as the controversial poet Irving Layton, the critic Milton Wilson, the shy pornographer of the Eastern townships John Glassco, and a horde of shadowy luminaries — poets and literati — he would seek his audience in *Playboy* and *Esquire*, not in little magazines in which poets write for other poets. His instinct, I believe, was poetically right, not commercially motivated. He had grasped what remains surely one of the major directions of contemporary or post-modern writing, its determined anti-literary, anti-humanist impulse.

To put the issue between modern and contemporary as one between the literary and anti-literary in writing — or between elitist and mass culture — I realize will sound extraordinarily simple-minded. Yet the point is worth considering. The mythology of Olson's *Maximus* poems, after all, is personal, local and historical rather than literary, general, and timeless; W.C. Williams chooses to mythologize not Troy but Paterson, New Jersey; a procedure distinct from Pound's poetic archeology in the *Cantos* that give us a multi-layered hero, a Ulysses who has seen many cities, many men, who speaks not only the lingo of Williams' persona but the rhetoric of epic, romance, and lyrics. It is true, of course, that the same tension between a mythopoeic European culture and an experiential American one — between the fine and the crude as Warren Tallman would have it — underlies Walt Whitman's ironic demythologizing of literature and is explicitly recognized in Pound's line "I make a pact with you, Walt Whitman." It is also true that Northrop Frye's brilliant point about the technique of displacement enables us to understand that the real distinction is not between realism and mythologizing. Twain's river story repeats a story as old as that in Williams' *Paterson* and Olson's *Maximus*; the quest pattern of the one, and the city who is a giant man in the other two works, are as old as the Bible, if not older. But what structural principles tell us about is form, and though it is customary now to make light of content, the *interest* of the writer in the details of a felt life, as Henry James would put it, to abandon the habits of allusion, the manner of speech, the rhetoric, the profound familiarity of a whole culture, a way of being, could prove to be more significant than in our more rigorously aesthetic moments we might believe.

In short, to turn to Canadian examples, when Margaret Atwood chooses the photograph in place of the reduplicating images of the Persephone story, when Gwen MacEwen turns to magicians and peanut-butter sandwiches rather than the oft-told stories of Athens and Jerusalem, when Michael Ondaatje finds his text in forgeries of the legend of *Billy the Kid* and the methodology of spaghetti westerns, we can suspect not only that new literary techniques are being employed but that new sensibilities are demanding their own inventions. Robert Kroetsch speaks not only of uninventing the world but the two prior acts of imagination in what he takes to be a development of a post-modern sensibility: the first, naming, inventing the world; and second, re-naming or re-inventing it. The first great cataloguing of words, something like A.M. Klein's Adamic poetic activity, we recognize as a traditional version of poetic power of the sort modernists claimed for themselves.

> . . . Look, he is
> the nth Adam taking a green inventory
> in world but scarcely uttered, naming, praising,
> the flowering fiats in the meadow, the
> syllabled fur, stars aspirate, the pollen
> whose sweet collusion sounds eternally.
> For to praise
>
> the world — he, solitary man — is breath
> to him. Until it has been praised, that part
> has not been. Item by exciting item —
> air to his lungs, and pressured blood to his heart —
> they are pulsated, and breathed, until they map,
> not the world's, but his own body's chart!

And now in imagination he has climbed
another planet, the better to look
with single camera view upon this earth —
its total scope, and each afflated tick,
its talk, its trick, its tracklessness — and this,
this, he would like to write down in a book!

To find a new function for the declasse craft
archaic like the fletcher's; to make a new thing;
to say the word that will become sixth sense;
perhaps by necessity and indirection bring
new forms to life, anonymously, new creeds —
O, some how pay back the daily larcenies of the lung![8]

   The second prior act of imagination seems to me very
much the sort of mythologizing wonderfully achieved in
Canada in the work of writers of the 50's like Ann
Wilkinson, Wilfred Watson, James Reaney — and, I would
add, especially Irving Layton — those who took the
traditional and rooted stories of western mythology and
gave them a habitation and a name in those barren places
of our imagination — Western Ontario, Winnipeg, Edmon-
ton, Toronto and Downsview. A superb example is Layton's reworking of Greek myth and Nietzschian cultural
criticism in "The Birth of Tragedy", a poem that provides a
key to much of Layton's work. But that domestication of
myth, if it *is* more than a technical tour de force, provides
little more than an accomodation of contemporary experience to a long tradition of thought and feeling. I say
"little more," which perhaps betrays a bias. What remains a
mystery, I believe, is the point at which a literary mythology no longer serves its social functions. Too many
others have written off cultures and announced the death
of gods for anyone today to assume a prophetic mantle
easily, and the kinds of social questions raised about
technology and art seem to me far too complex for any
kind of answer within the terms of this discussion. But the
facts are observable and they extend at least to Kroetsch's
version that "post-modern" means erasure, unwriting, the
inversion of high and low culture. What we are to make of

that is I think the major question Cohen's work raises. Another way to put this is to return to a concern I pointed to earlier in his work, one that becomes acute as he turns from high to low culture in response to the demands of audience: what connections could there possibly be between the dream of art and the reality of history?

Empson somewhere talks of Swift's discovery that everything high has a gross and low parody of it, the discovery that Norman O. Brown describes in his article "The Excremental Vision" in *Life Against Death*.[9] Cohen's identification of his sources and audience and his exploration of their meaning is of the same order: a Keatsian ode can be displaced into the diction, imagery, and rhythms of contemporary mass culture. The point of connection between art and history is fantasy. The demands of art and audience can be reconciled when nightmare becomes popular song, high becomes low, low high. A brilliant foreshadowing of what such inversions mean is Cohen's identification of artist and junkie, "Alexander Trocchi, Public Junkie, Priez Pour Nous." It begins, as you know:

Who is purer
    more simple than you?
Priests play poker with the burghers
police in underwear
        leave Crime at the office,
Our poets work bankers' hours
retire to wives and fame reports.
The spike flashes in your blood
permanent as a silver lighthouse.

(*SP*, 108)

and continues with a contrast between Trocchi and the poet himself:

I'm apt to loaf
    in a coma of newspapers,
avoid the second-hand bodies
which cry to be catalogued.

I dream I'm
   a divine right Prime Minister,
I abandon plans for bloodshed in Canada.
I accept an O.B.E.

Under hard lights
with doctors' instruments
   you are at work
in the bathrooms of the city,
changing The Law.

I tend to get distracted
   by hydrogen bombs,
by Uncle's disapproval
   of my treachery
to the men's clothing industry.

I find myself
   believing public clocks,
taking advice
from the Dachau generation

The spike hunts
constant as a compass.
   You smile like a Navajo
discovering American oil
on his official slum wilderness,
a surprise every half hour.

(SP, 108-9)

The conclusion becomes obvious and paradoxical:

Your purity drives me to work.
I must get back to lust and microscopes,
experiments in embalming,
resume the census of my address book.

You leave behind you a fanatic
to answer RCMP questions.

(SP, 110)

The true artist — and saint — is the junkie: pure, focused, concentrated, craftsman of need.

The Trocchi poem prefigures *The Energy of Slaves* in theme and image but not in tone or method, and from that point of view it is not fully realized, a sensation rather than a real scandal. Between it and the genuine failure, something else had to intervene and that, of course, is *Beautiful Losers*. The point of this poetic novel is an ironic version of transformation: the ironic defense of the position of pop-hero, mass cult figure, is that he doesn't really exist; he has become an image, he has turned himself finally and formally into his art, he is a voice, a book, a radio, a vehicle spoken through rather than speaking. A neat trick, but unfortunately it didn't work. For whatever reason, *Beautiful Losers* seemed to both audience and critic confirmation of Cohen's mastery. Con-man, magician, scandal-monger, elusive charmer, he became more, not less evident, and all the flim-flummery of the book fooled no one. He had become that worst of all things, an artist. It is this double dialectic then, "poems that drove me into poetry" and "women who keep driving me back into it,"[10] that remains unresolved and that occupies Cohen once more in *The Energy of Slaves*, a book about poetry, about enslavement, about politics.

Embarassingly, the book raises a whole series of critical questions, many deliberately invited by Cohen himself, all of the most elementary kind, the sort usually handled with smug assurance by teachers of freshmen, the *Philistine* questions. Has he lost his talent? Or in a more vulgar form: is this poetry at all? Is this, as Cohen keeps insisting, the last feeble glimmering of a dying talent? "I'm no longer at my best practising/the craft of verse"; he writes — or "Poetry begun in this mood rarely succeeds"; "Do you like this song?/I wrote it in a mood/that I would never/be seen dead in"; "Perhaps it is because my music/does not sing for me"; "That's why I can't write it anymore/I couldn't take the company";[11] and of course the lines most often quoted:

I have no talent left
I can't write a poem anymore

You can call me Len or Lennie now
like you always wanted

(*ES*, 112)

Is poetry itself now impossible? Or in another series: are
there some feelings that are simply anti-poetic or non-
poetic? Self-pity? Hatred? Loathing? Disgust? Is there an
authentic poetic language? Is it possible to write poetry
about the impossibility of writing poetry? Is the dramatiza-
tion of inauthenticity authentic? Is a genuinely inauthentic
poem an authentic poem? And add to these: flat uninteres-
ting structures, limp lines, flaccid diction, with just enough
of a hint of the old lyric flair to reinforce the challenge to
one's taste in such matters. The great classical structures
of critical argument bear no relationship to this collapsed
lyricism parading its limpness.

Two matters remain and bring this discussion to a close:
one, the motif of slavery; the other, the assault on the
audience or reader or "you" spoken to in the book. Both
proceed, I believe, from the assumption of a betrayal
common to both reader and poet. The first need not
occupy us at length since it is the elaboration of the
Trocchi point: slavery is defined simply as art and addiction. Art is opposed to work; it is habit, need, no longer the
romanticized purity, focus, and concentration of the
Trocchi poem, but the routine dreariness of meaningless
necessary repetition. At the same time, the assault on the
reader involves not only the poet's denial of talent but the
reader's implication in the writer's own junkie world. They
stand in the relation of supplier to addict, feeding on each
other's morbid necessities:

Before you accuse me of boring you
(your ultimate triumph and relief)
remember neither you or me
is fucking right now
and once again you have enjoyed
the company of my soul

(*ES*, 112)

Another version of the dialectic appears: poet and audience, once in opposition to each other as art and history, now are coupled in opposition to life itself. This faked-up, hokey, tic-tackery of poems and songs, presenting itself as the imaginative revolution, calling on us to rouse up our faculties, now proves itself anything but the power of transformation. Its unity of being is seen finally as genitalia or mere mechanism of need, the unity of being hooked. The attack on culture implicit in the opposition between art and *real* wars, *real* love, *real* revolution is the more poignant in Cohen because he once believed in a perceptual revolution, because he once thought poetry was the front line, real politics. "This book," he once said of *Flowers for Hitler*, "moves me from this world of golden boy poet to the dung pile of the front line writer."[12] Now, his mastery consists in taking the machine apart, bolt by bolt, to reveal it never worked anyhow.

Perhaps Cohen's argument simply provides fuel for those who would burn the poet anyway: it turns out, after all, that he deals in commonplaces, cliche's of contemporary thought, the detritus of cultural criticism, his language uninspired at that. But to say this is to spring the trap about which Cohen has been warning all along, even in his style. A double bind exists: condemn him and you are on the side of a now impossible refinement; join with him and you admit your complicity. The context of *The Energy of Slaves* is audience and politics; the persona, slave; the object now appears, paradoxically, as mastery or freedom. To be poet-master without being a poet-master.

The point is worth some elaboration, since it marks out the characteristic role assumed by the contemporary writer, "For God's sake, don't call it art." One means to achieve this ironic position, I've suggested, is disorganization; another, shifting the field of reference from high to low, from elitist to popular forms; a third, perhaps the most subtle, consists of taking on any one of a variety of contemporary roles from junkie to madwoman to outlaw/ forger or confidence man. Duplicity is far more characteristic of contemporary writing than either writer or reader seems willing to admit. Atwood's "This is a Photograph of Me," for example, opens out to possibilities that remain extraordinarily disturbing, especially since as the first poem in her first book it announces an obsessive concern. The photograph, we are told by the narrator in the same tone used to describe apparently objective features, "was taken/the day after I drowned/I am in the lake, in the centre/of the picture, just under the surface."[13] What are we to make of this? That a drowned woman is speaking to us? That the camera has subsumed her soul, drowned her? That the narrator, whose tone is so at odds with the situation, is insane? Or that the poem itself is a massive deception built on ambiguities inherent in structure, exploitable in diction? Or to take one other brief example, Ondaatje's *Billy the Kid*, warns of duplicity in "photographs," exploits forgeries, anachronism, and deception; and his passionate, loving, and controlled meditation on a photograph of his adolescence, "Burning Hills," ends with the astonishing lines that offer, if not an explanation, at least the questions to be asked:

When he finishes he will go back
hunting for the lies that are obvious.[14]

What lies? *Only* the obvious ones? Are there others? Will any be changed or only discovered by the poet, left there for our own bemusement?

In *The Modern Century*, Northrop Frye links the criminal-saint and outlaw figure with a tradition in American pastoral, on the one hand, of the artist as hobo and bum, and in European romanticism, on the other, of artist as bohemian and confidence man, and I suppose, as Frye notes, Cohen's work belongs there, as does Atwood's or Ondaatje's. But to notice the traditional features of the role does not, I think, answer to its contemporary implications. Cervantes wrote in the 16th century at the very moment when, as Leo Spitzer observes, the power of literacy manifested itself in the new humanism.[15] One possible reading of the *Don Quixote* is as an ironic attack on the dissolution of reality in the medium of print. That Cervantes' attack on books is itself in a book is surely additional and intended irony. That the meaning of imagination has been a perennial problem for *writers* in no way lessens the significance of a contemporary critique of high culture. Given a particular technology, the ghost of Cervantes may have more, not less, reason for living today than at any time since he first wrote.

My point has been mainly to explicate, to put Cohen's book in the context of a culture which in part he helped to create. But I would go further: *The Energy of Slaves* remains valuable because it elucidates with the precision we used to call poetry the failure of contemporary poetry. Far more uncompromising than Lee or Atwood or Bowering or Ondaatje, and more scrupulous, Cohen is equally more compromised than all of them because closer to each of us, that is, to the duplicity of consciousness and history. His development as a writer illustrates, as it creates, one of the main lines of development in Canadian writing, the gradual realization that art has the capacity to contain its own contradiction. *The Energy of Slaves* has the inevitability of fated writing; it was inherent in Cohen's understanding of contemporary imagination (i.e. his audience) and his awareness of the infinite regressiveness of personality, "all this endless reconsidering,"[16] as Philip Roth says about novelists; it was inherent too, we can now understand, in the first words a young poet wrote about a drowned god or in the lyric lines about a clever corpse in a love-soaked bed or in the urging of an imaginative revolutionary like a manic P.M. in Cuba to his brothers to join him governing this country. That poem is called "The Only Tourist in Havana Turns His Thoughts Homeward" and I conclude with its splendid and lunatic anarchy:

Come, my brothers,
let us govern Canada,
let us find our serious heads,
let us dump asbestos on the White House,
let us make the French talk English,
   not only here but everywhere,
let us torture the Senate individually
   until they confess,

let us purge the New Party,
let us encourage the dark races
   so they'll be lenient
   when they take over,
let us make the CBC talk English. . . .
let us have another official language,
let us determine what it will be,
let us give a Canada Council Fellowship
   to the most original suggestion,
let us teach sex in the home
   to parents,
let us threaten to join the U.S.A.
   and pull out at the last moment,
my brothers, come,
our serious heads are waiting for us somewhere
   like Gladstone bags abandoned
   after a *coup d'etat*,
let us put them on very quickly,
let us maintain a stony silence
   on the St. Lawrence Seaway.

Havana, April 1961

(*SP*, 104)

[1] George Steiner, *Language & Silence* (New York: Athenum 1967), p. 10.

[2] *Ibid.*, p. 10.

[3] Northrop Frye, *The Modern Century* (Toronto: Oxford University Press, 1967), p. 85.

[4] *Ibid.*, p. 104.

[5] W.A. Johnsen, "Toward a Redefinition of Modernism", *Boundary/2*, Vol. II, No. 3, Spring 1974, p. 543.

[6] Robert Kroetsch, "Preface To Canadian Edition", *Boundary/2*, Vol. III, No. 1, Fall 1974, p. 1.

[7] Leonard Cohen, *Selected Poems* (Toronto: McClelland & Stewart, 1968), p. 57.

[8] A.M. Klein, "Portrait of the Poet as Landscape", *Collected Poems* (Toronto: McGraw Hill, 1974), pp. 334-335.

[9] N.O. Brown, "The Excremantal Vision", *Life Against Death* Wesleyan University Press, 1963), pp. 179-201.

[10] Leonard Cohen, *The Energy of Slaves* (Toronto: McClelland & Stewart, 1972), pp. 14, 112.

[11] *Ibid.*, pp. 24, 18, 56, 74, 107.

[12] Leonard Cohen, *Flowers for Hitler* (Toronto: McClelland & Stewart, 1964), blurb on back cover.

[13] Margaret Atwood, "This is a Photograph of Me", *The Circle Game* (Toronto: Contact Press, 1966), p. 11.

[14] Michael Ondaatje, *Rat Jelly* (Toronto: Coach House Press, 1973), p. 58.

[15] Leo Spitzer, "On the Significance of Don Quijote", ed. Lowry Nelson Jr., *Cervantes* (New Jersey: Prentice Hall, 1969), pp. 85-86.

[16] Ann Mandel, "Useful Fictions: Legends of the Self in Roth, Blaise, Kroetsch, and Nowlan", *The Ontario Review*, No. 3, Fall-Winter 1975-1976, p. 32.